Jorjette Brown

About the Author

Susan Forward, Ph.D., is an internationally acclaimed therapist, lecturer, and author. Her books include the number-one *New York Times* bestsellers *Men Who Hate Women and the Women Who Love Them* and *Toxic Parents*, as well as *Obsessive Love*, *Emotional Blackmail*, and *When Your Lover Is a Liar*. In addition to her private practice, she has served widely as a therapist, instructor, and consultant in many southern California psychiatric and mental facilities. She is in much demand as a guest in the media, and she hosted her own daily call-in program on ABC's *Talkradio* for six years. She maintains offices in Los Angeles, California. For further information, you can reach her at fsusanf@aol.com or visit her website at www.susanforward.com.

Do Your In-Laws:

- Steadily criticize or belittle you?
- Regularly turn to your partner to meet their needs?
- Make derogatory comments about your appearance, work, political or religious beliefs, or things that are important to you?
- Regularly give unsolicited advice?
- Criticize the way you raise your children?
- Make unreasonable demands on your time?
- Let you know you are unwelcome in their family?
- Drink excessively or abuse drugs?

If you have answered "yes" to any of these questions, you have in-laws who create chaos in your marriage and assume they have the right to control your life.

TOXIC IN-LAWS

Loving Strategies for Protecting Your Marriage

Susan Forward, Ph.D.

with Donna Frazier

Quill
An Imprint of HarperCollins*Publishers*

A hardcover edition of this book was published in 2001 by HarperCollins Publishers.

First Quill edition published 2002.

Designed by Brian C. Barth

The Library of Congress has catalogued the hardcover edition as follows:
Forward, Susan.
Toxic in-laws : loving strategies for protecting your marriage / by Susan Forward with Donna Frazier.
p. cm.
Includes index.
ISBN 0-06-019681-5
1. Marriage. 2. Married people—Family relationships. 3. Parents-in-law. 4. Parent and adult child. I. Frazier, Donna. II. Title.

HQ734 .F713 2001
306.81—dc21 2001024211

ISBN 0-06-050785-3 (pbk.)

02 03 04 05 06 ❖/RRD 10 9 8 7 6 5 4 3 2 1

Contents

TOXIC IN-LAWS

Introduction

In the idyllic days of courtship, you feel like you've reinvented love and you're about to create the kind of family you always wanted. That's the powerful vision that pulls us into marriage.

Early on it's easy to minimize the complex mélange of philosophical, religious, social, cultural, intellectual, and purely quirky differences that exist between you. Soon enough, though, there are holidays to be celebrated, rooms decorated, toothpaste tubes squeezed, investments made—and the differences that reveal themselves can test even the strongest relationship. The pushes and pulls that are part of every marriage would be stressful enough if the two of you had no one to deal with but each other. But the bewildering, scary, and often painful truth is that we don't marry just one person. We come into marriage with our own unique history, needs, and set ways of doing things, and we marry into a family with its own store of emotional baggage and tribal customs. We now have a mate. And, in most cases, we now have in-laws.

NOT ALL IN-LAWS ARE A PROBLEM

Some in-laws are really great, despite all the jokes and complaints. I know people with the good fortune to have wonderful in-laws, and I hope there is a special place in heaven for those parents who treat the new member of their family with affection and respect—feelings that deepen and enrich over time. I know several people who adore their in-laws, and several others who find their relationships with them more fulfilling than the ones they had with their own parents. I know others, who have in-laws that are real stinkers, but are protected by partners who keep the situation manageable by setting appropriate limits on their parents' behavior. They're lucky. But vast numbers of others have discovered that their in-laws are a serious source of conflict and friction in their marriage and their life.

This book is a vital guide for those of you who have discovered, or fear, that the very fabric of your marriage is being eroded and threatened by the resentment, frustration, anger, guilt, and hopelessness that your relationship with your in-laws creates. Faced with their criticism, coldness, or attempts to interfere in your life, you may wind up in sniping battles, or find yourself smoldering, yelling at your partner, or crying after every encounter. Or, perhaps, you've tried to smooth things over, smile, make nice, and pretend everything is fine. Out of love for your partner and a desire to not rock the boat, maybe you "go along to get along"—only to realize that you are repeatedly compromising your feelings, your beliefs, your desires, and, ultimately, some of your personal integrity.

There's no question that in-law problems grind you down. But, more fundamentally, they work directly to weaken the bonds that connect you and your partner—and the longer they go unaddressed or are allowed to escalate, the more damaging they become. In my more than twenty-five years of counseling both individuals and couples of all ages and types, one indisputable fact has emerged true and clear: *When you have in-law problems, you have marriage problems.* That's the bad news. The good news is that once you understand the complex system that connects you, your partner, and your in-laws, there are wonderfully empowering and effective things you can do to make the situation better—for yourself, for your partner, and for your life together.

WHO ARE TOXIC IN-LAWS?

First, let's define our terms.

In my book *Toxic Parents,* I wrote that I chose the word "toxic" with great care. I know how provocative the word is, but I was, and still am, convinced it is the best word for describing the erosive and poisonous effect that certain people in our lives can have on us. And as you will see throughout this book, toxic in-laws honed their skills as toxic parents.

Toxic in-laws are more than just occasionally annoying or difficult. They are more than people who don't meet your dreams of how in-laws should be. You may find your in-laws' taste to be tacky, or their politics unpleasant. You may squirm around them because you feel you have so little in common. But discomfort and social awkwardness alone don't mean you've got toxic in-laws.

Toxic in-laws are people who, through various types of assaults on you and your marriage, create genuine chaos. These assaults can be open and aggressive or subtle and subversive. They may range from attempts to control you through guilt-peddling or the use of money, to hurtful rejection of you because of religious or cultural differences. They are usually unapologetic and often unrelenting.

Please note that when I use the term "toxic in-laws," I am referring specifically to your partner's parent or parents. I know that many of you may have great difficulties with other in-laws as well—an obnoxious brother-in-law or a backbiting sister-in-law, but there is a unique power imbalance built into the adult-to-adult-child relationship. The older generation is invested by culture and society with both authority and an expectation of respect, whether they have earned it or not. Also, because they are, in most cases, from the same generation as your own parents, they often activate many of your unresolved parental conflicts.

DO YOU HAVE TOXIC IN-LAWS?

To pinpoint toxic in-laws, it's helpful to look at two areas: (1) conditions in your in-laws' own lives that make them more likely to interfere in your marriage, and (2) actual evidence of harmful intrusions. The following checklist can help you identify trouble spots:

Do Your In-Laws:

1. Have a cold or volatile relationship with each other?
2. Fight a great deal?
3. Drink excessively or abuse drugs?

4. If widowed or divorced, resist making a new life for themselves and expect your partner to be a surrogate spouse?
5. Regularly turn to your partner to meet their needs?
6. Regularly set up situations in which your partner is forced to choose between your needs and theirs?
7. Regularly criticize one or both of you?
8. Make derogatory comments about your appearance, work, political or religious beliefs, or things and people that are important to you?
9. Bribe you and your partner to get what they want?
10. Consistently try to make you and/or your partner feel guilty if you say "no" to them?
11. Constantly give unsolicited advice?

If you've answered "yes" to even one of the first three questions, your in-laws are highly likely to play out their personal problems in your marriage. One or two "yeses" on items four through eleven indicate that you already have problems with your in-laws that need some attention. And if you've answered "yes" to three or more of those questions, you have toxic in-laws who assume they have the right to control major areas of your life.

As obvious as their problem behavior is, your in-laws may be totally unaware of its impact on you. Sometimes their actions simply reflect the way they are and have always been. And quite often, those actions are invisible to your in-laws because no one has ever let them know how much unhappiness they are causing.

In the first half of this book, we'll look not only at what your in-laws are doing, but what they hope to accomplish—the one underlying goal that unites all toxic in-laws. We'll also look at how their actions trigger you and your partner, and at the difficulties that arise when your partner is torn between love for you and a lifelong loyalty to his or her parents.

YOUR IN-LAW SURVIVAL MANUAL

In the second half of the book, I will help you navigate when the seas of toxic in-laws get really stormy. First, I will teach you compassionate ways of dealing with a husband or wife who can't or won't stand up to their parents. I'll show you surefire ways to defuse the sense of betrayal and frustration that flare up when a partner (1) doesn't protect or defend you from his or her parents, or (2) becomes upset when you try to protect or defend yourself.

Then I will guide you through the process of reclaiming your marriage from your in-laws, whether or not your partner will work with you. I will teach you what to say, what to do, what limits to set, and what kind of expectations are reasonable and realistic.

But dealing with in-laws is not just a matter of being assertive and letting them know what they're doing to you and what you want from them. In everyday life, they'll do things that upset you and make you angry (just as your parents may frequently affect your partner in the same way). But being an assertive person doesn't mean you need to go to the wall with them on *everything* that bothers you. I'll teach you how to be less reactive when they push your buttons and how to decide what behaviors you must deal with.

REALITY AND ACCEPTANCE

I can't promise you that this book will magically erase all the differences between you and your in-laws and leave you with the relationship you've always wanted. What I *can* do is help you put an end to much of the damaging behavior, then create—and live with—the best connection that's possible between you and them. It may be painful to put aside dreams of closeness when your in-laws won't allow it, but there is a great peace that comes from recognizing what *is* rather than constantly longing for more and resenting those who can't give it to you.

Those of you who have read some of my other books know that I have always been willing to share my personal struggles with you. I hope it helps you to feel safe with me to know that I have experienced many of the same things you have, and have made many of the same mistakes.

You may also be surprised to find that the centerpiece of the work we'll be doing in this book won't involve confrontation so much as something I've come to value highly—realistic acceptance. I'm not suggesting for a moment that you passively accept behavior that is clearly unacceptable. But I am suggesting that if you look carefully at your unrealistic expectations and what you bring to the conflicts with your in-laws, you may see the outlines of an emotional map that you have the power to change.

In my own life, there has been a tremendous internal struggle to give up the litany of "I'm right, they're wrong" and the self-righteous satisfaction that comes with that perception. I have learned, through the pain and error that so often create wisdom, that people can only give what they can give and can only be who they are. We are all limited in certain ways, and we are all the product of our history. I have learned that it's better to be with even limited people in a calm and loving way rather than be alienated. Realistic acceptance has made my life infinitely better.

You can let go of the resentment that is not serving you well and find the peace that comes with a realistic assessment of what can and can't be in your relationship with your in-laws. This, in turn, will allow you to be with people in a different way that, in itself, draws a more open reaction to them.

PRACTICAL ANSWERS TO UNIVERSAL DILEMMAS

I know that you will have many questions, and I will help you find the answers to the ones I have heard the most often about toxic in-laws. Questions like:

1. My husband gets really angry when I tell him I don't want to spend time with his parents. Do I have the right to upset everyone?

2. How do I deal with my guilt if I don't just go along with what everyone else wants?

3. The problem is between my in-laws and me. Can't I just deal with them without involving my wife?

4. My in-laws get their digs in at me when my husband isn't around. He thinks I'm exaggerating and oversensitive. How can I get him to take this seriously?

5. My father-in-law ruins every get-together with his drinking and obnoxious behavior, but how can I tell him not to come to our home?

6. Aren't I being petty and selfish if I expect my husband to put me first?

Step by step, I will help you deal firmly and compassionately with toxic in-laws, and give your marriage room to breathe.

THE POWER OF POSITIVE DOING

One of the most popular books ever written is *The Power of Positive Thinking*—a wonderfully inspirational guide. I'd like to show you how to take positive thinking to the next plateau—to the power that comes from changing behavior and actively taking steps to deal effectively with a difficult situation. It takes courage and determination, and armed with new clarity and new skills, you will find the inner strength you need.

You can reclaim a marriage battered by divided loyalties. In most cases, you can make peace with your in-laws. You certainly can make peace with your partner and with yourself. Positive thinking is wonderful, but positive DOING will genuinely change your life.

I know that many of you have been feeling hopeless and helpless in your relationship with your in-laws. But the situation is far from hopeless and you are certainly not helpless. There is much you can do. You have the power to change your own reactions to what's going on, and, as you do, you will see and feel differently. You will create changes in the people you love—and the ones you hope to. What have you got to lose?

PART ONE

Toxic In-Laws

1

The In-Law Triangle

By the time you reach the point of a serious commitment, you usually know a lot about your partner, and you've either met or heard about the family, with all its saints, smotherers, dictators, and martyrs. Looking back now, with the dazzling clarity of hindsight, you can probably remember your first inkling that you were headed for in-law trouble. For some people, it's a frosty reception or a sense of tension that never seems to lift. For others, the preview of things to come flashes past in curt phone conversations and cutting remarks. If the unpleasant moments dissipate and don't form lasting patterns of behavior, there's no major problem. Other times, however, there's a revealing moment or event that signaled the beginning of ongoing trouble, and you can play it back in your mind like a movie.

For Anne, a thirty-one-year-old graphic designer, it was

her prospective mother-in-law's reaction to a personal and professional decision she made.

"Ruth started on me even before Joe and I got married. She was incensed that I wasn't going to change my name, even though it's on all my business literature and phonebook ads. At the rehearsal dinner, she told Joe, loud enough for several people to hear, including me, that, in her opinion, I'm too ambitious and he'll be playing second fiddle to my career, which, of course, is worthless as far as she's concerned—even though she has a career of her own. I didn't say anything, but I felt humiliated and furious. So I tried to laugh it off and make nice. It just wasn't the time for an argument."

Joe's mother was critical and denigrating with Anne, and her behavior was a bright-red flag. Should Anne have reconsidered marrying Joe because of it? Of course not. But certainly if Ruth's behavior persisted, there were things Anne and Joe would need to address between them, and issues for the two women to resolve as well.

Over time, though, Anne could never find the "right time" to work things out. Four years into her marriage, when she came to see me, she was still feeling humiliated and furious—and berating herself for shrugging off those early warning signs and permitting Ruth's behavior to go unchecked. Like most people with toxic in-laws, she'd sensed from the beginning that marriage would turn out less like a happy merger of two families than a hostile takeover by her partner's parents. But working against that realization were the potent forces that keep many of us suffering in silence. You're in love. You don't want to bring up anything that could spoil the romantic feelings. You want to be liked and accepted by your future in-laws.

Anne looked back in amazement at how hard she'd worked to persuade herself that the unpleasantness at the rehearsal dinner was a momentary blip—followed by years of new "momentary blips":

"I wanted so much for her to like me, and I was sure that she would once she got to know me, but that was a laugh. After we got married, it only got worse. Then I was sure that things would improve after she became a grandmother. Now it's two grandchildren later, and she's still taking potshots at me all the time."

Why do we so often let months and years pass between the time we know we have in-law problems and the time we stop waiting for them to disappear on their own? I'm convinced that it's because we cling to a whole collection of reassuring platitudes about how best to handle in-laws. These reassurances are deeply etched into our collective belief systems, and they crop up often in the advice of well-meaning friends and relatives. They're the first things we tell ourselves when we realize, with a thud of dread, that our current or future in-laws aren't our allies. I call these beliefs "In-Law Myths," because most of the time they are pure wishful thinking and not grounded in reality. They are comforting, though, and we cling to them until they're as threadbare as an old security blanket.

CUTTING THROUGH THE IN-LAW MYTHS

The seven short statements that follow sound perfectly reasonable, and like tall stakes in a garden, they serve as supports for the tiny shoots of hope, which, over time, bloom into a thicket of lulling beliefs and rationalizations. Holding on to any of these myths will keep you from focusing on what is happening right now in your relationship with your in-laws. So, though I know it may leave you feeling vulnerable, I'd like to dispel these fantasies, one by one.

1. Things Will Get Better After We're Married.

They might. They might also get worse. As the wedding day comes and goes, most people find that toxic in-laws are consistent. If they didn't warm to you while you were dating, and even worked on their son or daughter to break up with you, it's highly unlikely that they'll drop the campaign against you while you wait for them to come around. Wedding cakes and rings are lovely and meaningful symbols, but they're not magic when it comes to solving in-law problems.

2. Things Will Get Better After They Get to Know Me.

This phrase echoes poignantly among people struggling to cope with the hurt of in-law criticism or rejection. Time and familiarity alone won't open closed hearts and minds. Putting on a brave front while waiting for your natural goodness and charm to win them over is like waiting for a broken dish to mend itself.

3. Things Will Get Better Once I Have a Baby.

Certainly I've seen cases of in-laws who softened considerably once they became grandparents. But don't count on it. It's possible that even if they warm to the new grandchild, those good feelings will not extend to you. And if they firmly believe they know what's best for you and your partner, you can be sure they will also know what's best for your children. After all, they're parenting pros, and you're an amateur.

Don't be surprised to discover that in creating a new life you've also created a new arena for conflict.

4. If I Do What They Want, They'll Have to Like Me.

Keep in mind that pretending to agree about important differences or giving in to pressure to get your in-laws to approve of you may work in the short term, but over the long haul it rarely does. Some in-laws will keep raising the bar until you are faced with a demand you can't comply with. Still others will come to accept the false, compliant you and never know the real person behind the "peace at any price" mask. You can't win in any of these scenarios, or emerge with your self-respect intact.

5. They're Not My Parents, So How Much Can They Bother Me?

The answer is: Plenty! If they're extremely possessive of your partner, it will affect you. If they disapprove of you and let your partner (and often you) know it, it affects you. If they invade your life in any of the several ways that we'll explore in the following chapters, you will not escape the fallout. And if all of that wasn't enough, in-laws have a way of reactivating old insecurities and hurts handed down from our own parents because they are authority figures from the same generation.

6. They Live in Another State, So We Won't Have to Deal with Them Very Much.

Last time I checked, long-distance rates were dropping by the minute, and for just a few hundred dollars you can fly almost anywhere. In some ways, your relationship with your in-laws can be more difficult if you see them infrequently, because weeks and months of emotion are packed into a condensed period of time. Living far from your in-laws may mean that you don't spend much time in their house, or they in yours, but it hardly means that they won't be a regular presence in your life.

7. My Partner Will Always Put Me First.

Probably true—until it comes time to deal with his or her parents.

I've seen every one of these myths endure—typically, as in Anne's case, in the face of ample evidence to the contrary. They pop up like life preservers when you feel the deep pain that comes with rejection and hostility. They seem to calm you down when you're ready to strangle your mother- or father-in-law, and they create the illusion of "giving you perspective" when you're feeling raw after a contentious encounter with your partner's folks. But, in truth, they only keep you from seeing clearly, responding smartly, or taking effective action when problems arise. Let's switch our focus, then, to reality. It may not always be what you hoped for, but it's still the only game in town.

REALITY, PART ONE: HOW TOXIC IN-LAWS BEHAVE

In the chapters that follow, I will ask you to look closely at how the most typical kinds of problem in-laws behave. I'll take you through an exploration of their preferred actions, their tactics, and what appears to be motivating much of their treatment of you. It's been my experience that most people don't bother to step back and study their in-laws' actions because it seems so futile. The reasoning goes: I didn't choose them, I can't divorce them, I can't really hire someone to get rid of them, and we all know you can't change other people—so what's the point? As a result, you may be paralyzed by a sense of hopelessness over the intensity of your emotional reactions to your in-laws without ever really engaging your reason to look at what they're doing and how it affects both you and your partner. Worse, you may perpetuate their patterns of behavior with predictable responses that unknowingly give your in-laws exactly what they want.

I'm sure you'll see your own in-laws among:

The critics, who view you as incompetent or character-flawed because you have different ideas, preferences, belief systems, values, or ways of doing things. This category includes the scapegoaters, who blame you for whatever problems you and your partner may be having.

The engulfers, who view your marriage license as enlistment papers, signing you up for total involvement with them.

The controllers, who believe that your partner is incapable of handling his or her own life and step in to do it better. Controllers demand compliance and offer their very conditional variety of love on the basis of how good a job you do of pleasing them.

The masters of chaos, who've done little or nothing to control their addictions, marital conflicts, and financial problems, creating havoc that draws in your partner and spills over into your family.

The rejectors, the deliberately hurtful in-laws whose cruel, angry, often abusive behavior is deeply painful and almost always involves active attempts to sabotage your marriage by turning your partner against you.

These categories aren't always discrete and neatly separated. Many of the in-laws you'll see straddle several of these groupings, being critical at some points, for example, engulfing at others. Most, however, fall back on one particular mode in their dealings with you and your partner, and it's the most prevalent behavior that we'll focus on. The stories you'll hear about each of these in-law types will help you see into the workings of your partner's parents, and through them, you'll gain much of the clarity necessary to move toward change.

IT TAKES THREE

What makes in-law problems especially difficult to manage is that they're part of a three-way system, a triangle.

Obviously, you wouldn't have in-law problems if you'd married into a family of happy, tolerant people with full lives and big hearts. It's equally true, however, that you'd probably be able to successfully manage your differences with even the worst in-laws if your partner were willing to stand up for you and put your well-being above his parents' preferences. I promised you that we'd replace the in-law myths with reality, so let's turn our attention now to the other key players in toxic in-law relationships: Your partner and you.

REALITY, PART TWO: THE PARTNER PROBLEM

What happens to some people when they're in the same room as their parents? Many of you have found, to your bewilderment, that the strong, competent man you married turns into a scared little kid around his parents, or that confident, spirited woman you fell in love with is guilt-ridden and subservient with hers. If you thought you were marrying someone who would always be on your team and follow through on the plans you had made together, seeing that person crumble around your in-laws can be a shock.

For Hope, a twenty-two-year-old receptionist, that shock came just before the first Christmas she had looked forward to spending with her fiancé:

"I'd heard all about Jerry's parents while we were dating. From what I can tell, they hate each other, but they still live in the same house. They've got separate bedrooms and, basically, separate lives. The father won't go anywhere and just putters around at his workbench in the garage. He's the king of the cold shoulder—especially to his wife. Jerry's mother is really lonely and so she's always looked to Jerry, who's an only child, for companionship and closeness. They've done a lot of traveling together, and he escorts her to the theater—that sort of thing. Anyhow, it was our first Christmas together and we'd made plans to go to Hawaii—and his mother calls. She tells Jerry she's made a lot of money in the stock market and she wants to take him to Europe, since it will probably be the last trip they'll be able to go on together—because of me, of course. At Christmas! Just the two of them! Jerry couldn't understand what I was so upset about."

For Tim, a thirty-eight-year-old graphic artist, it was a rainy Saturday four months into his marriage:

"We were lying in bed and I asked Tracy how she wanted

to spend the day. She got up to open the window and, with her back to me, she said something about having to straighten up the guest room for her parents. I thought I couldn't have heard right, because our deal is that friends use the guest room and family stays in a hotel. That's what happens with my folks, and I assumed we were going to do the same with hers. Tracy told me her parents would be offended if they thought we didn't want them to stay with us, and, like an idiot, I gave in. Her mother spent the week scrubbing the toilet and trying to reorganize the house, and her dad, after putting away half a bottle of scotch, gave us nightly lectures about how extravagant we are and how to handle our money. We couldn't get away from them. It was a nightmare."

And from a woman who wrote to Dear Abby, a snapshot of real trouble ahead:

"Dear Abby: I am a 32-year-old divorcée who is soon to be remarried, and already I am having trouble with 'the in-laws.' I have never encountered people so rude in all my life. They refuse to have anything to do with me.

"My fiancé's parents were cordial and friendly to me until I began dating their son. Then came the dirty looks and rude behavior. Abby, I have never done anything to offend these people. Even my fiancé agrees that I have done nothing wrong.

"His mother said point-blank to me, 'You wait until someone steals your son and see how it feels!' I realize that there might be some sadness that her 'baby' has decided to leave the nest, but, for heaven's sake, the 'baby' is 26 years old and has a mind of his own. This is nature taking its natural course.

"It has been a year and a half, and they still will have nothing to do with me. However, they expect their son to come home and visit, and he does. I am angry that he goes there knowing full well how they feel about me. What should I do?"

Each of these people was facing different in-law troubles: a lonely, dissatisfied parent competing for attention; the first of endless hours of unasked-for advice; a woman who views her prospective daughter-in-law as a usurper and villain. But what they all have in common is a partner who, for reasons that often seem incomprehensible, is unwilling to take a firm stand and actively set appropriate boundaries on his or her parents' behavior.

The sting in that lack of support is often far more hurtful than anything your in-laws themselves can do. My client Anne expressed the resentment, frustration, anger, and sense of abandonment that almost all of us experience when our partner won't become our ally in dealing with our in-laws:

"He won't stand up for me, and he gets real defensive when I try to talk to him about what's happening. I think he's scared of his mom. I think he's always been scared of her. I feel totally betrayed—like I'm all alone and there's no one in my corner. I'm at the breaking point—he's beginning to seem like a total wimp to me. I don't even know where to start dealing with this. Do I yell at him, tell his mother to shove it, get a divorce, or get an ulcer? I thought Joe and I could get through anything together. . . . Who's he married to—me or her?"

If you feel as though you're in the middle of a powerful tug-of-war for your partner's loyalty, you're right. And if you think you're at a disadvantage in this battle, you're right again. Sometimes, with little more than a word or a glance, your in-laws can call up and activate decades' worth of loyalties, rules, shoulds, and feelings about "the way things are supposed to be." They set in motion patterns that are so familiar to your partner that they feel like gravity—invisible, inevitable, and unalterable.

In the chapters ahead, as we examine how different types

of toxic in-laws behave, I want you to look carefully at how your in-laws maneuver your partner to get what they want. A good deal of their power depends directly on your spouse, the gatekeeper who knowingly or unknowingly gives them permission to put their stamp on your life. That means many of their efforts will be aimed at keeping your partner from growing up, becoming emotionally emancipated from them, challenging them, and protecting you.

Understanding just how your in-laws are affecting your partner will help break through the anger and bafflement that make conflicts over in-laws so painful. If you are using this book alone, it will help you look at your partner's behavior with less bitterness and more empathy. And if you are sharing this book with your partner, it will give him or her a valuable starting point for first seeing, then changing, the parent-child dynamic.

REALITY, PART THREE: WHAT YOU BRING TO THE MIX

As difficult as it is to acknowledge, you have your own role to play in the in-law drama. Your expectations and your responses to encounters with your partner's family set the emotional tone for your dealings with them, and though those emotional colorings may be invisible to you, they're often what your in-laws see and respond to. And, sometimes, what they see is not at all what you think you're offering them.

As we move through the pages to come, you'll have many opportunities to see the actions and reactions of people who, like you, are trying to cope with the behavior of toxic in-laws and unsupportive spouses. While looking at their responses, I think, you'll begin to see how the problems that come from the outside can remain unresolved and even intensified by our own overreactiveness and unrealistic expectations.

Let me show you what I mean about what you may be putting into the stew:

Leslie was twenty-eight when she first came to see me, frightened and depressed that her four-year marriage to her high-school sweetheart, Tommy, was being destroyed by her husband's parents.

Leslie is a bright, vivacious young woman who had been a successful stockbroker for several years. I learned that she had come from a very chaotic and emotionally abusive family. Leslie had overcome a great deal to attain professional success, but she still had many uncertainties about herself.

At Tommy's urging, she gave up her work to help him in his family's enormously successful printing business. But from the beginning, Tommy's parents had been overtly disapproving of the marriage.

"Tommy's from this large Italian family, and I thought, Oh, good! I had this terrible childhood, but maybe I get a second chance at having a family. Maybe now I'll get the family I always dreamed about."

Many of us have such high hopes for what marriage will bring us in addition to the partnership—a new chance for family, warm, loving parents like the ones many of us didn't have—that we are totally thrown off-balance when that doesn't happen.

"I was the first girl he ever took home to meet his parents. Tommy was working in the family business and living at home. The first thing that happened was, I took off my shoes when I came in their house, because they had this thick, white carpeting and I didn't want to get it dirty. Tommy's father said I was rude and had no manners. They constantly criticized me, even though I did everything to try and get them to like me. I brought them flowers and little presents, but nothing I did made any difference. They told Tommy I wasn't 'one of them.' "

The behavior of Tommy's parents was absolutely bewildering to Leslie. Their responses to her were completely out of proportion to anything she may have said or done. They were critical of Leslie before they even had a chance to get to know her. But nobody called them on their behavior and nobody set limits on what was and wasn't acceptable. Instead, Leslie slipped into a familiar and comfortable role—one that she knew well.

Over the next few years, Leslie continued to see herself as a victim of both Tommy's parents and Tommy's silent compliance. Yes, Tommy's parents were critical and unloving much of the time. And yes, Tommy was unprotective and weak with them. But there's more going on here than a simple case of victim and victimizer.

Leslie came into her relationship with the unrealistic expectation that people with whom she had neither history nor emotional connection would fill up the emotional void left by her own parents. And when that failed to happen, she bristled at everything that sounded like criticism and got caught up in an endless loop of frustration, hurt, and disappointment.

Then, in an attempt to understand what was going on, Leslie did something with her in-laws' behavior that was even more self-defeating—she turned it into further evidence of her own unworthiness:

"I wanted those people to love me so much. So when they didn't, I took it to mean there's something terribly wrong with me. Well, that was a familiar feeling—that made everything make sense."

As we worked together, Leslie came to see just how much

she brought to the table—a damaged self-image, a heightened vulnerability to criticism, and the ease with which she slipped into the victim role. None of this excused or justified her in-laws' behavior, but because of her own insecurities, she had few skills that would have allowed her to stand up for herself and handle conflicts differently. Fortunately, as you will see, both Leslie and Tommy were able to make major changes in their relationship and in the way they dealt with Tommy's parents, which put their marriage back on track.

THE MARK OF HISTORY

The eagerness to please and be accepted by the new family is natural and understandable—up to a point. When those needs cause you to behave in self-defeating ways, they become part of your contribution to the problems, no matter what your in-laws may be doing.

We all come into marriage shaped by our emotional history. There is no question that your partner's experience in his or her family will determine how active and protective he or she will be with you when there are in-law problems. But as you've seen with Leslie, your own self-image and confidence will play a large role in how you react to your in-laws' behavior—and how much they learn they can get away with.

THE LINE THAT TOXIC IN-LAWS CROSS

That said, I want you to keep one last, crucial rule firmly in mind:

Your in-laws are required to treat you with courtesy and respect. This is minimal and nonnegotiable.

The toxic in-laws we're about to meet consistently violate this basic tenet. Their dislike and discomfort are expressed overtly as disrespect for you and your spouse. Even if their interference in your life is disguised, and their aggression is passive instead of blatant, all have crossed the line into behavior aimed at chipping away your partner's loyalty to you. All of them use any resources at their disposal—their wealth or neediness, their lifelong claim to your partner's love, their age or authority—to keep their child controlled, and, at their worst, to undermine the independent adult relationship between you and your spouse.

As you watch them at work, remember that you are looking at a system of interactions. Pay attention to how each side of the triangle affects the other, and keep an eye out for the in-law myths and what happens when couples get lost in them.

I know that many of you have already identified with some of the people you have met so far, and will continue to do so as we go on together. I also know that reading about what other people have gone through lets you know that you are not alone. You are not the only one in the world who feels the way you do, and you're certainly not the only one to whom these things have happened. There is an incredible clarity that comes from this type of exploration, which is the crucial first step toward the wonderful changes that are in store for you.

2

The Critics

Critics are the in-laws who look upon almost every interaction as an opportunity to scrutinize your opinions, feelings, and actions, weigh them against their own, and find you lacking. Whether their aim is to lash out, exert their superiority, or simply mark their territory, they almost reflexively do it with blame, disapproval, and put-downs aimed at letting you know that you just don't measure up to their standards or expectations. When they disagree, they won't let the issue rest. They harp. They pick. They "advise." They nag.

Like all negative behavior patterns, criticism covers a spectrum that can range from annoying to wounding, which is to say that not all critical comments are destructive, or even terribly problematic. If most of your in-laws' criticisms strike you as small-minded, old-fashioned, or just plain silly (they make fun of your old Toyota or make disparaging remarks about your wearing jeans to go out to dinner), it won't do you any lasting harm to let the comments pass. This is especially true if your relationship with your in-laws is basically sound, and the criticism is sporadic or not cruel, even though they can't help reminding you from time to time that they know best. You can probably wave them away like gnats, keeping your sense of humor. I know that sometimes you'd like to retaliate with a few choice words, but in dealing with these essentially nontoxic in-laws, you can almost always find a creative strategy for getting your message across.

My friend Erica, for example, found that she didn't have to bring out the heavy artillery to silence her mother-in-law Ruth's constant criticisms of her driving:

"Ruth is in her late sixties now. I admire a lot of things about her and I enjoy her company—most of the time. She's witty and interested in the arts, but she's a little on the compulsive side and wants things done her way. She doesn't like to drive at night, so I'll take her out to the movies or to dinner, especially if my husband is working or out of town. But she's the worst backseat driver you've ever seen. Except that she's in the front seat, so her criticism is harder to ignore.

"From the minute we get in the car, she starts. 'Why are you taking this street, there's too much traffic, you need to slow down, you're too reckless, we're going to miss the beginning of the picture, why don't you take the shortcut'—you get the point . . . I know it sounds petty and I should just ignore her, but it makes me really tense—and asking her to stop does no good at all. I used to just stuff my resentment and end up having a lousy evening because I was so pissed off. So one night I decided I had to do something about it."

Erica was wise to respect her personal limits. Perhaps

someone else could have just tuned Ruth out and let the nagging roll off their back, but Erica was not able to do that. Rather than letting her irritation build until it exploded, damaging what was basically a solid relationship, Erica came up with a solution that allowed her to feel much less stressed.

"The next time it happened, I just pulled over to the curb, turned off the ignition, handed her the keys, and said sweetly: 'Since you obviously don't approve of the way I drive or my choice of route, I think *you* should drive.' When I started to get out of the car to go around to the passenger side, she said, 'OK, OK—I get the picture. I know I have this terrible habit of trying to control everybody's driving—I did it with my husband, too—it's almost automatic. I promise to watch it.' 'And,' I told her, 'I promise to call you on it when it gets out of hand. Deal?' "

This is what's possible when the parties involved are reasonable people, both coming from a position of good will and actively doing something to resolve a minor conflict. Erica changed her characteristic way of handling the situation by deciding she wasn't willing to continue stuffing her annoyance and letting it spoil the evening for her. And Ruth not only owned up to her annoying behavior, she also made a genuine effort to modify her criticisms of Erica's driving. She valued their relationship and recognized that her nagging criticism about something relatively unimportant was affecting the good feelings between them. As with all bad habits, she regressed from time to time. But if she didn't catch herself, Erica gently reminded her of their agreement.

I know you may be rolling your eyes and thinking that your in-laws wouldn't possibly respond reasonably if you gently called them on their behavior. But keep these filters in mind before you decide:

- Is your relationship basically sound? Does the pleasure of the relationship generally outweigh the irritation?
- Are the criticisms petty and irritating, or are they intended to hurt you?

You may be surprised at how easy it is to make an oblivious in-law aware of criticism and help him or her change it. One good technique for deflecting nonassaultive criticism is to simply say something like: "And your reason for telling me this is . . . ?" This puts the ball back in the critics' court and puts them on the defensive as they struggle to explain why they found it necessary to make critical comments in the first place.

WHEN CRITICISM HITS A NERVE

We've been looking at best-case scenarios, the relationships that can be tolerable, and much better, if we can keep things in perspective, remember that we're adults, and give our in-laws some mild coaching when irritations threaten to get out of hand. But very few of us can manage to stay calm and centered when what's in the crosshair of an in-law's criticism is something close to the heart: the value of what you do, the wisdom of your life choices, your worth or attractiveness as a person, the quality of the love and care you give your partner or your children. Toxic in-laws seem to have built-in radar devices to locate our most sensitive hot buttons. It's not our driving or cooking they zero in on: It's *us*.

With assorted styles and weapons, they hit us where it hurts. They may use cruel words, delivered with heat and ham-fisted directness. Their critiques of us may also be hushed, even silent, or masked behind helpfulness or generosity. It's easy to slip into mythical thinking ("They'll change when they get to know me better," "They're just trying to help") until we look directly at their behavior, so let's turn our attention to the varied MO's and guises of the problem critic.

THE ALTRUISTIC CRITIC

Altruistic critics will tell you that they have nothing but your best interests at heart. If they challenge your decisions, try to change your way of doing things, or impose their preferences and routines on you, they'll justify their actions with words like:

- Can't you see I'm only trying to help?
- Can't you see how much I love you?
- Can't you see that I want to make things easier for you?
- Can't you see that it's for your own good?

It's difficult to "see" any of those things, of course, because in truth, "loving" advice you didn't ask for and "caring" interference in your affairs inevitably feel like what they are: criticism.

Cal, a thirty-two-year-old contractor, thought he'd found an ally, even a friend, in his wife's father, Ray, a businessman who'd built his own house.

"Ray seemed like such a cool guy when I first started talking to him. He knows a lot about building, and he seemed really interested in what I do. So when Karen told me he wanted to come over and help me convert the garage for her office, I said sure. Turns out, the guy is a total know-it-all. I stained the doors for a closet, and the next day he had them off the hinges, doing them over and telling me my work wouldn't pass a junior-high shop class. I couldn't believe it. I do this for a living, and he's saying I'm holding the hammer wrong! He said he'd help me get done faster, but as soon as I do something, he's shaking his head in disapproval and actually taking the tool out of my hand and saying, 'Here, let me show you how to do it.' I'm ready to wring his neck, but Karen thinks he's the hero. He sure makes it look that way."

As Cal discovered, the altruist critics can transform any offer of help into an exercise in self-aggrandizement, a way of building themselves up at your expense.

Cal's wife, Karen, added fuel to the fire by buying into her father's altruistic pose:

"Frankly, I think Cal is being a big baby. Daddy's doing such a nice job on everything—sure, he's a perfectionist, which drives Cal crazy, but the results are so great. I'm getting this gorgeous office, just what I wanted. Cal's so busy, and Daddy has more time to take care of the details—what's the problem with that?"

The problem was that Ray became highly competitive with his new son-in-law. It's not unusual for a father to want to show his daughter that he is more of a man than the new husband—smarter, stronger, more competent, more successful. In my work with Cal and Karen, I learned that Ray rarely missed an opportunity to seize any opening to undermine Cal in Karen's eyes, usually in the name of "helping" and "making things easier."

And Karen, who had always adored her father, couldn't see the validity of Cal's complaints. She consistently sided with her father, which angered Cal even more, and simply didn't recognize how strained the family relationships were becoming. When Cal decided he had to confront Ray, she begged him not to do anything that would "hurt her father's feelings." Unfortunately, Cal's feelings didn't seem to be as important to her.

GRANDMOTHER KNOWS BEST

An all-too-familiar example of the altruistic critic is the in-law who uses the birth of a grandchild as a never-ending opportunity to demonstrate his or her superiority at the expense of the vulnerability of the new parents.

My client Rita, a lanky thirty-four-year-old event planner, vividly recounted the steady stream of criticism she got from her mother-in-law.

"At first, Vivian seemed so well-meaning. She loved the baby—he's the first grandchild—and she was very generous with money and gifts. She came over a lot to help out, even with the cleaning. But, somehow, she thought that gave her the right to criticize almost everything I did—and not just once in a while—it was relentless. If I picked him up when he was crying, she'd say, 'You're fussing with him. You're overstimulating him. Just let him cry himself to sleep.' That may be what *she* did, but it's not what *I* wanted to do. Then she was appalled that I had decided not to nurse him, and said that I was being totally selfish, and everything she's read indicates that children who are nursed are far better adjusted, and I was depriving my baby of a good start in life, as if I hadn't done any research on my own. When it comes to Alex, she's the expert. I'm the idiot. I'm going to ruin little Alex, and she's the one who'll save him."

With critical in-laws you'll never do it right, and, yes, you're scarring the poor baby for life. In casting themselves as experts and even saviors, they tell us in actions and words,

"I know best. I can do it better. I know how to raise babies—and you don't."

Everyone is anxious about their first child: Am I doing it right? Am I doing something that will traumatize him? Though it was a long time ago, I can still remember how horribly inadequate I felt with my first child, and my self-doubts made me hypersensitive to any and all criticism.

Even if the in-law is less overtly critical than Ray or Vivian, the altruist's unsolicited advice carries with it an enormous amount of criticism, which frequently infuriates the recipient. It's not friendly, it's not loving, and it's generally not even well-intentioned. Its purpose is simply to demonstrate the critic's superior knowledge, skill, and adequacy.

WHEN YOUR PARTNER DOESN'T GET IT

Just as Karen couldn't understand why Cal was so angry with her father, Rita's husband, Lee, also had trouble understanding how adversely his mother's criticism, masquerading as helpful advice, affected his wife.

"My mom's been so good, spending all this time with the baby and giving me and Rita a break. I know she has her own way of doing things, but I came out OK, didn't I? My mom feels really unappreciated. This thing is really getting out of hand. Rita's sulking half the time . . . I know my mom can be picky, but that's just the way she is. She means well, and I don't know why Rita is being so cold to her."

Lee was only focused on a part of the picture—tuning into his mother's seemingly positive messages—"Look how much I'm doing for you, look how it's for your own good," "I'm just trying to help"—while tuning out the obvious or implicit criticism that was so painful to Rita.

WHAT YOU CAN AND CAN'T ACCEPT

It's a tough balancing act, dealing with altruistic critics, because on the one hand, their help and contributions may be welcome. But if the one-upmanship in their agendas and the way they belittle you becomes a pattern, you can't just bite your tongue and keep quiet. You pay too great a price in mental and emotional health if you don't set appropriate limits on hurtful behavior. I don't advocate that you go to the mat every time a piece of advice is offered. But there's a big difference between unsolicited advice and demeaning criticism that is a direct attack on you, and it's important to step back and determine just what's coming at you. You have the right to actively deal with criticism that hurts or denigrates you, even if your partner continues to rationalize and excuse everything by insisting, "They're only trying to help."

In the second part of this book, I'll show you some truly effective strategies for dealing with altruistic critics. You'll learn how to acknowledge their help while drawing a very clear line that they may not cross.

THE TWO-FACED CRITICS

Some in-laws criticize in very devious ways. They may:

1. Criticize you when your partner isn't around and act reasonably pleasant to you when he is.
2. Criticize you to your partner and put on a pleasant face when you're in their presence.

Either way, their sniping creates tension and major misunderstandings in your marriage.

Pam, a twenty-seven-year-old artist who designs store-window displays, felt pelted by her mother-in-law Sylvia's "private" comments.

"I hate those times she comes over and Chris is working late. One of her favorite routines is, 'Don't you think it's time you thought about children? You're not getting any younger, you know. I had three children by the time I was your age.' Or she'll pull out her compact at the dinner table and put on more lipstick, then turn to me and whisper, 'You're too pale. You need to wear more makeup, dear.' Like it's her way of bonding, to criticize me. She doesn't let up when we're alone together, but she's all nice-nice when Chris is around. She'll send him off so 'us girls' can clean up the kitchen, and then light into me about how untidy my kitchen is. Chris acts like he doesn't believe me when I tell him what she says. And to add oil to the fire, he tells me I'm being too emotional. Then I start to wonder if maybe I *am* being too sensitive. Why can't he see that I need his support with this, and not criticism from him as well?"

As a result of Chris's indifference to his mother's behavior, Pam felt very alone. She knew she was not being heard or understood. Ultimately, she withdrew into angry silences instead of finding appropriate methods to counteract Sylvia's behavior.

CRITICISM BY PROXY

When you give someone your proxy, you are authorizing them to act on your behalf. In-laws who criticize by proxy use your partner as their representative to avoid the discomfort of taking you on directly. Instead, they often come in smiling, cloyingly pleasant packages. To look at the way they act when you're together, you might not regard them as critics at all. Maybe you sense their disapproval, and maybe they seem a little stiff and phony, but, you reason, that's certainly not the same as an attack on you. As you're about to see, however, their artificial pleasantness is often a cover for the criticism they're letting fly when you're out of their presence.

An all-too-familiar "criticism by proxy" strategy is practiced by the critic I call "the injustice collector." These critics fill up their bag of resentments with imagined slights. Injustice collectors distort many of the things you do and say and see them as personal attacks. But instead of dealing directly with you, they pull in your partner when they want to vent their criticism of you.

Angela, a twenty-two-year-old legal secretary, discovered that her mother-in-law, Frances, was a master of this type of distortion.

"Last Thanksgiving we had the family over. I was in the kitchen, and Frances and Ed were setting the table. I could hear Frances telling Ed that she's deeply offended by my attitude to her, especially on the telephone. She said that every time I answer the phone and I hand it to Ed because she's asked to speak to him, I say, 'It's your mother'—which is absolutely true. And I'm thinking, 'What on earth is the problem?' Well, it seems, she's convinced I'm being, in her words, 'insulting and dismissive and not showing her proper respect,' and she told Ed he should get me to be nicer to her. He mumbled something about how he'd try. I couldn't believe what I was hearing."

Angela's bewilderment was understandable. It's often very difficult to figure out how an injustice collector can misinterpret even the most benign remark or bit of behavior and experience it negatively.

But at least overhearing the exchange between her husband and his mother opened the door to some new honesty between Angela and Ed.

"After everyone went home, I told Ed what I'd overheard and asked him what else his mother complains about, because she sure won't do it to my face. He tried to brush it aside, but I could see he was really squirming. I told him I'd always sensed a real chill from her, and he and I needed to deal with this. He agreed and said he was really tired of being put in the middle. He said his mother bristles at many of the things I say and has been complaining about my 'rudeness and lack of respect' almost from the time I came on the scene. If he defends me to her, she becomes very quiet and withdrawn. So he feels he can't win."

Ed was right—he couldn't win the way he'd been handling the situation. All he could do was make it worse. Frances was trying to use him as the means to change behavior in Angela that she found objectionable. I told Ed that he was letting himself be manipulated into a position very much like that of a referee in a prize fight trying to intervene between the two opponents. Who did he think got clobbered in those circumstances? He needed to let the two people involved find a way to resolve things. His job was to refuse to be put in the middle and refuse to carry his mother's complaints home to Angela.

Injustice collectors love to complain about the person they believe has hurt them to everyone but the person involved. The incidents they criticize are often petty and ridiculous, but to them even minor incidents are a federal offense. They often play the role of victim/martyr to the hilt and prefer to get other people to do their dirty work for them—usually their child, your partner.

THE ANIMOSITY RUBS OFF

My client Pat, an energetic forty-two-year-old makeup artist, was badly shaken when she realized the erosive effect her in-laws' criticism was having on her marriage:

"I noticed that every time Jeff came back from a visit to his parents—he goes up to Santa Barbara a couple of times a month to see them—he was incredibly nasty to me when he got home. Totally different—he hated how I cooked, what I was wearing. Nothing I could do satisfied him. It would take him days to calm down and get back to normal. It was like being married to two different men. It didn't take a rocket scientist to put it together—that something must be going on with his parents. So I asked him point-blank: 'What are they saying to you?' And it turns out that they're totally tearing me apart to him. They go through the whole list: She's too self-centered, she's irresponsible with money, she thinks she's better than everybody else. Christ, by the time they're done he doesn't know what to think. And these are the people who are so icky-sweet to me when we're together!"

I told Pat that her in-laws were using Jeff as the agent of their negativity and criticism. Unwilling to express their criticisms directly to Pat, they attacked her through Jeff. In that way, they could convince themselves that they weren't responsible for hurting Pat's feelings and that they weren't really doing anything harmful.

THE GOOD BOY

In couples' counseling with Pat and Jeff, it soon became clear that Jeff's role in his family had always been "the good boy":

"My parents always had very high expectations of me. I don't see what's wrong with that. I had to get *A*s, be a star athlete, sing in the church choir. . . . I loved it when I knew they were proud of me."

Who wouldn't! But there was a lot of pressure on Jeff, and those smiles of approval and pride quickly turned to critical disappointment if he fell short of their expectations in any way:

"I'll admit, if I goofed up I never heard the end of it. . . . I hated it when I thought I'd let them down."

Fast-forward to the present: Jeff knew his parents wanted him to marry the daughter of a wealthy family friend, and he showed a lot of backbone by choosing someone else. But, unfortunately, despite that show of independence, he slipped back into his familiar role once his parents started attacking Pat. Jeff believed he had no choice but to listen. Good boys don't argue or disagree with their parents. Jeff's early programming as the golden child, the one who does what his parents want, was stronger at those times than his loyalty to Pat. It was as if he had exhausted his supply of courage once he got through the wedding.

If his parents wanted to criticize Pat, he would listen. If they wanted him to go home and dump on her, he would. He would continue to be the good boy until it almost destroyed his marriage.

Up until the time we began working together, Jeff was almost oblivious to how much his parents were still influencing his thoughts, feelings, and behavior:

"I actually thought I was absorbing a lot of the negativity—at least Pat didn't have to listen to it. I know I'm usually in a bad mood after I see my folks, but I didn't realize just how awful I was being—I really thought I was protecting her."

THE CRITICISM DIDN'T START YESTERDAY

Of course, Jeff could put an end to a lot of this behavior by insisting that his parents stop criticizing Pat behind her back and getting out of the line of fire. But as I suspected and he substantiated, Jeff, like many people who become ineffectual with their parents, had been conditioned by years of exposure to his parents' criticism. He had never been able to protect himself when he disappointed them in the past. Now he had disappointed them again by his choice of wife. As a result, when they switched their sniping to Pat, this was familiar territory for him.

When critics go after you while your partner isn't around, it can be expedient for your partner to gratefully grab the excuse to plead ignorance.

"I never heard a mean word from my mom when she was around Pat, so I just couldn't see why Pat was so upset. You should see them together. Mom fusses over her, she's always saying nice things—but Pat just pulls away."

Your partner may not see what you see, or easily feel what you feel, when your in-laws snipe at you. He may seem to spend inordinate amounts of time and energy trying to provide the "context" for their behavior, or "helping you understand" why you shouldn't take offense or defend yourself. And though you could cut it with a butter knife, your partner may not accurately pick up on the tension in the room between you and your in-laws because that's what he or she grew up with and has become used to.

WHEN CRITICISM TURNS TO SCAPEGOATING

Scapegoating is criticism taken to the next dimension, in which your in-laws not only find fault with you, but also blame you for everything that goes wrong in your marriage, in your partner's life, and in the lives of your children. They may even assign you the responsibility for discord in the extended family, and a whole rainbow of situations that are clearly beyond your control.

Fran, a thirty-one-year-old high-school teacher with large gray eyes, became the scapegoat for, of all things, her child's health problems:

"Libby, my oldest daughter, has allergies and asthma, and my father-in-law is constantly telling me that we're not getting the right help for her. The asthma has really stabilized, but Jake blames me for the fact that she's sick at all. The treatment's not good enough. The doctor must be wrong because I chose him. I wish Libby didn't have asthma, but she's a happy child and she's doing fine. Jake just can't see that. He believes somehow that I did this to her!"

Loving in-laws would give you empathy and offers of help if your children have health problems, but scapegoaters like Jake use such trying and difficult times to knock you even further off balance, intensifying the feelings of guilt and inadequacy you already have. As absurd as it may seem, I've seen in-laws blame their children's partners for everything from hyperactivity to dyslexia and emotional problems that have a multitude of causes, including biochemical imbalances, which are nobody's fault. And they're generally far less interested in understanding the situation than in using it as another weapon.

PUTTING ON CONVENIENT BLINDERS

Some in-laws use scapegoating to shield themselves from difficult truths about themselves and their children. They may be perfectly friendly until something happens to challenge their carefully erected defenses.

Catherine, a petite thirty-year-old accountant, found herself becoming a scapegoat when she began having problems in her marriage to Sam, a difficult and increasingly abusive musician.

"At first, Mona and Harold were both thrilled to have me in the family, because I was ambitious and responsible. But soon after we were married, Sam, who'd been so exciting and interesting when we were dating, turned into another person. He became incredibly jealous and moody. He didn't like my friends, he would become furious if I liked a piece of music he didn't approve of—I never knew what would set him off. I didn't want to burden my own parents with this, because they were going through a rough time financially, so I confided in Mona. I think Harold knew what was going on, but he was pretty passive and just went along with whatever Mona would say. . . . I couldn't believe Mona's reaction the first time I asked for her help in understanding what was going on with Sam. I thought she would be sympathetic—after all, she knows what he's like—but when Sam and I had a fight, she always said it was my fault because I didn't know how to handle him and was too demanding and unsupportive—even though he was getting more and more verbally abusive and his anger was getting scary."

Sam's parents had an enormous blind spot where their son was concerned, and no matter how nice they seemed to Catherine, they instantly sided with their child—Mona actively and Harold complicitly, instead of taking her concerns about Sam's behavior seriously.

"She told me that I had to find ways to get along with Sam because he was an artist. I had to understand that he was just 'sensitive,' and 'very emotional.' She acknowledged that he'd been a difficult child, but, according to her, it was his volatile temperament that made him special. I, on the other hand, was in the 'business world,' and my values were all warped—that's what she said—conveniently overlooking the fact that I supported us when Sam couldn't find work. She even told me that I needed to go into therapy so I could learn to be more loving and accepting!"

Sam's parents had created a romanticized image of their son that allowed them to deny the fact that Sam was an unstable and potentially violent young man. If they had stopped criticizing Catherine long enough to look in the mirror, they might have had to face some very uncomfortable realities about their offspring. As difficult as owning up to those truths would have been, it would have allowed Catherine's in-laws to ally with her in intervening with Sam, and possibly being a force for steering him toward some much-needed help.

Unfortunately, they were locked into their denial. After all, if they acknowledged the truth, what would that say about the job they had done as parents? How could they live with the guilt of knowing that they might have created a rotten kid? How could they justify to themselves that they didn't get him medical and psychiatric help when he manifested signs of problems early on? It was much more comfortable to look *outside* for an explanation. Far better to turn what could have been painful self-criticism into criticism of Catherine.

Sam, of course, was only too relieved to have all the problems in his marriage transferred to Catherine's shoulders. He could then avoid taking any responsibility for what was wrong or painful or even inexplicable in his life, as his parents had always allowed him to do.

Don't be too surprised if your partner goes along with his

or her parents and agrees with them that certain problems are "all your fault." In fact, the more dysfunctional your marriage, the more this is likely to occur. Your in-laws' scapegoating of you may be very seductive to your partner. It's always easier to point the finger of blame at somebody else to justify your own inadequacies.

A DANGEROUS PATTERN

Scapegoating can cause you to start doubting your perception of reality. It's difficult to hold on to what you know is true when such important people in your life are lined up against you.

In chapter 1, you saw how Leslie was temporarily swept along on the tide of "everything that's wrong in this family is Leslie's fault," and how she began to accept that as reality. When she did, she became a coconspirator in her in-laws' attempts to demonize her.

The darkest scenario for scapegoating can be seen in cases involving physical abuse. The parents of the abuser will typically gloss over the violence and blame their daughter-in-law for a variety of "character defects" that, they rationalize, caused the abuse or provoked it. In many instances, they will even accuse her of lying about it.

THE TARGET'S DILEMMA

And what about the targets of criticism? It's pretty bewildering to see people who are strong, smart adults respond to in-laws' criticism by seething silently or acting helpless.

I'm sure you're wondering by now why the targets of critics we've met don't do a better job of taking care of themselves. Why don't they say something at the time? After all, they're adults with rights of their own, and they shouldn't always expect their partner to run interference for them.

Many of us shrink from confronting our toxic in-laws because, faced with a partner's parents, we often don't feel like equals. These people have come into our lives not only in the role of family but of elders as well. It's common to feel strong social pressure to not offend them, even though they often seem to be doing their best to offend you.

"I DON'T WANT TO BE THE FAMILY VILLAIN"

Rita put her finger on some of the underlying forces that keep many people from responding effectively to an in-law's criticism:

"Yes, everyone knows my mother-in-law is a meddling pain in the neck, and I would love to tell her just that, but there seems to be some kind of unspoken rule that you just don't take her on. This is a family that likes to keep a very civilized veneer on things. I don't want to be the heavy, the one who sets her off and upsets everybody. So it's easier to just go along."

Rita acknowledged that she was perfectly capable of making her irritation known and taking steps to deal with criticism from a friend or colleague, but dealing with her mother-in-law involved much higher stakes and many more potential consequences. Not wanting to rock the family boat and be the identified troublemaker is a powerful silencer for many people.

AT A LOSS FOR WORDS

A lot of us also stay silent because we get tongue-tied when we are hurt and angry and can't think of anything to say.

That's what happened to Cal when his father-in-law was so demeaning to him:

"I have a lot of people working under me and I communicate just fine with them. But I swear to you, Susan, when that guy starts on me, I feel like I'm five years old, and I can't think of a damn thing to say to defend myself. My stomach is like a pretzel, and I can feel this tight band across my chest. . . . Sometimes I think I'm going to explode."

Few people have developed the skills to find the right words to say under pressure—words that will both empower them and defuse the tension in the atmosphere. Instead, our anxiety takes over, and we either blow up and declare war, or are so wounded we want only to retreat. How many times have you been irritated with yourself because you thought of something really terrific to say an hour or a day after someone offended you? It's a perfectly normal reaction—it's tough for your mind to work clearly when your stomach is tied up in knots. That's why you will find the scripts in the second half of this book so valuable. Once you learn your lines, you'll be able to say them no matter how nervous you get.

THE TUG-OF-WAR

There was another factor that kept Cal from taking any positive action—his wife's concern about offending her father. Many targets of critical in-laws will stuff their resentments in order to keep from upsetting or testing their partners. The situation may be bad, but like Cal, many people will sacrifice a lot of their dignity rather than upset their partner and their in-laws.

Rita also found herself in a tug-of-war:

"I don't want to put Lee in a position of having to choose

sides—of having to decide where his loyalties are. Maybe I'm scared that's a battle I won't win."

Rita was afraid to test Lee's priorities. She sensed that if he were asked to take sides, based on his previous reactions to Rita's complaints, he might very well have sided with his mother. The pain of her mother-in-law's criticism was less intense than the feared pain of her husband's betrayal. So, Rita, like so many people with toxic in-laws, decided not to take the risk.

From the outside, these reasons may not seem very persuasive. But from the inside of the cobbled-together family that marriage creates, they're some of the most powerful forces for maintaining the status quo, even when it's unhealthy for everyone concerned.

THE HIGH COST OF CRITICISM

Critics trigger many of our vulnerabilities and self-doubts. They chip (or blast) away at our confidence. If you're vulnerable to their barbs, you'll soon find yourself doubting your own perceptions and judgment. You may find yourself wondering: What if they're right? Could what they're saying really be true? Hearing exterior voices making negative judgments about you can strongly reinforce the self-criticism that we all struggle with. In the worst-case scenario, you'll end up doubting your ability to do anything right, and question your very worth.

It's easy, at that point, to silence the critics by doing things their way, and handing them increasing amounts of control over your life.

3

The Engulfers

Where critics amplify and invent flaws and weaknesses in you and your partner, engulfers are happy to acknowledge your goodness, your irreplaceable contribution to the family. They want to be with you, and they invest you with the unique ability to make their lives better. But these are the in-laws who measure your love in terms of time spent with them—and more is never enough. In their eyes, your needs for privacy, or just for time apart, are subordinate to their claims on your life.

Yet even as you sense that your in-laws are beginning to swallow your marriage whole, engulfment can be powerfully seductive. It frequently wears the guise of love, and it speaks in words that are freighted with longing for many of us: Connectedness. Love. Family. Tradition. What could be wrong with any of those things?

It may take a while to realize that for engulfing in-laws, these warm terms come cloaked in a very particular set of definitions and behaviors:

"Connectedness" means "You are not a separate person, and you come when I call."

"Love" means "You're my whole life, and it's up to you to make me happy."

"Family" means "Loyalty and first priority to your family of origin and not the new one you choose to make."

And "tradition" is "The unchanging law: We do what we've always done, no matter how your life has evolved."

Figuring out that you, your partner, and your in-laws have entirely different expectations when you talk about love and family may be a years-long struggle. Eventually, though, it becomes obvious that engulfers, no matter how warm and affectionate their demeanor, are like all toxic in-laws: They will be happy only if you and your partner go along with the program and put them first.

A FAIRY TALE WITH NO FAIRY-TALE ENDING

Liz, a thirty-year-old child-care aide with a tired face and a voice so soft I had to strain to hear it, came to see me on the recommendation of her doctor.

"I'd been having migraines for the first time in my life, and after he did every test in the book and found nothing, he turned to me and said, 'OK, Liz, what's bothering you?' And the first thing that popped out of my mouth was 'My goddamn mother-in-law'—something I never thought I'd say."

Liz told me that she came from a troubled family where there was little affection. As an adult, she yearned for a close-knit family, and couldn't believe her good fortune when she met Paul and, later, his family. She thought she'd died and gone to heaven:

"These people talked to each other. They spent time together. They need each other—they actually say "I love you" to each other. My god, they had family softball games and picnics. They included me in everything. It was fabulous—at first. Well—you know what they say, if something seems too good to be true, it usually is. You know how some people complain their in-laws are cold and distant? I'm now at the point where I would welcome a little distance."

Liz acknowledged that despite all the good things Paul's parents did, she was becoming increasingly concerned about how much time her new in-laws, especially Paul's mother, Terry, expected to spend with them. Terry had filled their life with invitations and activities before the wedding, but Liz had hoped that once she and Paul were married, Terry would begin to accept that Paul now had a life of his own, separate and distinct from her. As is so often the case, however, the more things change, the more they stay the same:

"I hate to sound so whiny when they've been so great to me in so many ways. They've really embraced me and certainly didn't object to our marriage, but they act like everything's supposed to be just the way it was before I came into the picture."

I asked Liz to tell me what was happening during this first year of their marriage.

"Terry's always letting Paul know that he's not spending enough time with the family—mainly, her. She concocts these family get-togethers and expects us to drop everything and attend. She even wants to double-date with us every weekend, like we're all a bunch of teenagers. The worst pressure came when we were planning our vacation. We're both nine-to-five people, and we only get two weeks off a year. But

Terry has gotten into planning these big family vacations—calling every day with a new trip idea, sending me brochures on cruises that the whole family could take together! I told Paul, I'm not spending our only two weeks with your family—we need time to ourselves. But then his mom said that if we didn't want to spend our vacation with them, they wouldn't go either, because they wouldn't enjoy themselves without us. So what was I supposed to do—I couldn't fight everybody. . . ."

Your in-laws' apparent generosity and excitement about including you may mask the clear demand that they attach to every seemingly flattering request for time and attention. But once they make you and your partner responsible for whether or not they have a good time, or even whether or not they're happy, you've moved out of the realm of closeness and togetherness into the dangerous arena of being the caretaker of their feelings. And that's such a heavy burden that, even if you're like Liz, and hungry for family connection, you'll inevitably want to pull away.

YOU WIND UP AS "THE PROBLEM"

Your shifting perceptions of your in-laws may strike your partner as an inexplicable mood swing. Liz's husband, Paul, was mystified and even angry as Liz tried to gain a little distance from his engulfing parents:

"I don't know what happened. She was so crazy about my family, and all of a sudden they're 'smothering' and 'demanding.' My mom was so hurt when Liz said she wanted to change our vacation plans. She didn't know what hit her, or what she did wrong. They love her—what's wrong with wanting the family to be close and together? I guess this is what happens when you've come from a really screwed-up family. You don't have any idea about what a real family is supposed to be."

Paul convinced himself that Liz's resistance was all a result of her troubled past. That made perfect sense to him and enabled him to avoid having to look any further at what might be going on in his own family and in him.

Naturally, Liz was hurt, even outraged, by Paul's response. It was extremely upsetting for her to see her marriage being manipulated by overly demanding in-laws, especially when Paul saw their behavior as perfectly normal. This was what he had grown up with, what he knew. There was no way he could understand how different his parents' expectations looked to Liz. And to make matters worse, Liz was losing a lot of respect for Paul, who turned into a doormat when his mother put sufficient pressure on him. Not surprisingly, Liz and Paul had a miserable vacation and were constantly sniping at each other. The good news is the trip precipitated their coming in for counseling.

WHY SHOULD MARRIAGE CHANGE ANYTHING?

A lot of in-laws seem stubbornly unable to understand that when their child marries, life will, of necessity, change. Many in-laws will fight tooth and nail to keep the "minor disruption" of your marriage from disturbing their old familiar patterns. And as you've already seen with the couples you've read about, and may have discovered for yourself, your partner may not be willing to rock the boat by changing those patterns, either.

Pete, a twenty-eight-year-old insurance salesman, came in full of frustration and anger over "how my wife is keeping us joined at the hip to her father." He knew that Ellen was extremely close to her father, Art, but he was amazed at how invasive Art became on an almost daily basis.

"You should see the way Art behaves with Ellen—like she's still living at home. He's always been superindulgent and overprotective with her. When she was in high school, he tried to get some teacher fired because he'd given Ellen a *C* in his course. Now, he calls her almost every night and asks her what we had for dinner, what we bought, how much money she made that day on commission. He won't let her leave the nest. He wants to be the first one she talks to any time she has to make a decision—even if it's something about us. He can't stand that she's no longer completely dependent on him. It's gotten to the point where I have to go into another room when she's talking to him—I just get so ticked off about how much her dad babies her. He won't let her be an adult—let alone a wife."

Art acted as if he viewed Ellen's marriage as, at most, an inconvenience, and continued to treat his daughter as if she were still a member of her original family. Her new family barely existed, as far as he was concerned.

But, as always, the in-law's behavior is just one part of the picture. Look at the interesting phrasing here from Pete: "He doesn't let her be an adult." When I asked Pete if he could express that in another way, one that would assign some of the responsibility to Ellen, he thought for a minute and then said with a deep sigh: "Yeah—I see what you mean. Ellen lets her dad keep her from being an adult."

Art's possessiveness with Ellen could only continue because she hadn't changed her own view of herself, and continued to feel more like a daughter than a wife. Like many young adults, Ellen experienced her marriage and her new independence as less real, less valid than the lifetime she had spent as her parents' daughter. Things would change when Ellen was able to understand that herself.

A GIFT-WRAPPED TRAP

By insisting that the ultimate family virtue is closeness, engulfers give themselves license to intrude into every aspect of your new life together. Some engulfers want to be so much a part of your life that you'll naturally be reminded of them wherever you look. And they're often completely oblivious to how invasive their presence is, and how destructive it is to the integrity of your marriage.

Leslie quickly found that her in-laws turned from nasty to devouring:

"Once they saw they couldn't stop the wedding, they changed their tune, and that seemed like an improvement. Suddenly, Tommy's mom wanted to be with us. Initially, she wanted us to move into their home on the pretext that it would help us save money. I thought she was kidding—I mean, what century are they from? But she didn't see anything odd about it at all. When I said 'No, thanks,' she insisted on going shopping with us to pick out furniture, and she said they'd pay for everything. I hated what she picked out, but Tommy said, 'How could we say no to a gift like that?' Gina told us what color to paint our apartment. She would come over unannounced with pictures she thought we should put up. All in the name of helping, of course. At first, I was so glad I'd finally gotten into that charmed circle. It was a lot better than being out in the cold. But now I feel like that character in the Bible who got swallowed by the whale. I think she wanted our place to look just like theirs. I think she wanted Tommy to feel he was still living at home."

A more accurate description would be that *her mother-in-law* wanted to feel as if Tommy was still living at home.

Tommy had found someone he really cared about and with whom he wanted to build his own family. But instead of being happy about these changes, Gina, who'd always leaned heavily on Tommy for emotional support, viewed Leslie as a frightening competitor. I told Leslie that she had run smack up against the intense primal connection between parent and child. In a healthy family, this connection is fluid and flexible and can adjust to change. But if your partner has a truly engulfing parent like Gina, the new person is seen as having lured away their life's blood, and gifts or offers of help often become a way of enticing their lost child and winning back his or her loyalty. The house and furniture episode was only the beginning of her efforts to drag Tommy back home.

CULTURE CLASHES

It's especially difficult to resist being pulled into the engulfing arms of your partner's family if you marry into a different culture, race, or religion. In the effort to be liked and accepted, many people bend over backward to understand and be tolerant of their new in-laws' customs. You may be unaware, at first, of just how much will be asked of you, and in the name of politeness and respect for your in-laws' traditions, you may go along with escalating expectations, only to find yourself growing increasingly resentful.

Kate, a twenty-three-year-old exercise instructor, fell in love with Ted, a businessman from a close, Jewish-Iranian family.

"When we were dating, and even when we were living together, I wasn't bothered by how much time we spent with Ted's family, but as soon as we got married, Ted informed me that we're supposed to have dinner with them every Sunday and every holiday. And the family is huge, including several people who don't even speak English. If I balk or Ted tries to tell them we have other plans, there's a lot of arm-twisting that goes on. They switch to Farsi sometimes when I'm around, and I feel like a little kid who's being talked about in code. What they believe is that family is everything and you don't need friends because friends are strangers."

Ted's parents even found a way that appeared generous and loving to override Kate's resistance to not spending important holidays with her own parents:

"When I brought up that I always have Thanksgiving with my parents, and perhaps we could alternate each year, they invited them, too. So now they've pulled my parents into this mess, and Mom and Dad don't want to be there—it's really boring for them. They want to have holiday dinners in their own home, and they're complaining to me and saying things like, 'So does this mean we never get to see you again on holidays unless we come over here?' and I've got stomach pains, which, my doctor said, is anxiety and tension. I just want everyone to be happy, and it seems like no one is ever satisfied."

I told Kate that her last statement wasn't quite accurate. Her in-laws were satisfied and probably assuming everyone else was, too. They would undoubtedly be astonished if anyone told them that their insistence on ritualistic attendance every weekend and holiday, with no room for compromise, was actually smothering and creating a lot of disruption. In their minds, they were being inclusive and embracing, and no one had the courage to tell them otherwise.

YOUR HOUSE IS THEIR HOUSE

Engulfers respect neither emotional nor physical boundaries, and there are few boundaries as meaningful as the four walls of your home. Your house is your haven, your domain, your personal territory, and engulfers ignore the sanctity of that territory when they:

- Come over without calling first
- Call without regard to the hour or your schedule
- Offer your home for family events without checking with you
- Insist on staying with you when they visit even though there are other options available

As irritating as the first three items may be for you, it's the fourth that really creates havoc. It's one thing when your in-laws drop in on you unannounced for the evening because they just "happened to be in the neighborhood." It's quite another when they expect you to accommodate them for long periods of time—weeks or even months, disrupting your routines, imposing their preferences, and demolishing your schedule.

THE INVADERS

Diane, a department-store buyer in her late forties who has two grown children, came to see me a week before the semi-annual visit of her in-laws, stressed and anxious.

"John's parents retired early and they have plenty of money, but their life consists of going from child to child, staying about a month. This has been going on now for about ten years. It's our turn, and I'm a wreck. I'm always tied in knots before they come because there's so much tension when they're here. I'm no good without my own space and privacy. They're OK people, but they've got their own little routines that are totally different from ours. Dinner at five, then they watch TV with the volume turned up beyond the threshold of pain, and, of course, they don't want to impose, but they do expect us to spend time entertaining them and taking them around. Honest to god, I don't know what my rights are here. After all, they are his parents and I should be able to just accept their visit, and if it were a few days I'm sure I could, but I wouldn't let my best friend stay for a month. We're both basket cases by the end of one of these visits."

Of course, Diane had plenty of rights, and there were numerous options for putting up her in-laws somewhere else, but she was too afraid of upsetting John and looking cold and uncaring, to exercise them. One obvious solution was to find a pleasant place for her in-laws to stay instead of with John and her. I told Diane that I was sure she had explored other alternatives.

"There's a charming new boutique hotel three blocks from us where they could stay, but as soon as John suggests it, they remind him of how welcome they are at his brothers' and sister's, and he backs down. His father wrote us a note in the Christmas card they sent that said, 'Since my heart attack, I've gotten my priorities straight, and my priority is family.' That's all it takes for John to lose whatever resolve he had to put them up somewhere else. I'm about ready to kill him."

Everybody's feelings were being taken into account but Diane's. If John's parents were hurt and offended by the suggestion that they stay somewhere else, then, of course, they would stay with John and Diane. And if John couldn't stand the guilt he felt for not allowing his parents to stay with their son and daughter-in-law, well, then, of course, Diane would just have to understand and couldn't possibly expect him to make other arrangements.

Engulfers have the power of history on their side. If they've been very enmeshed with their children, your marriage doesn't change that. Even though John was an independent lawyer, close to fifty, his father still was able to invoke that early bonding and remind his son of how much he and family meant to him. John's parents looked on their visits as a way of deepening their connection with their son. They often talked about their children as their best friends and rhapsodized about how lucky they were to have such an open, loving relationship with them. It was easy for John to forget that there was little actual openness in his family. The unspoken truth among his siblings was that their parents' visits were a terrible imposition. And, for Diane, the stays were a sure route to migraine headaches and overwhelming stress.

Engulfers gain a lot of their power from knowing that their adult child has an overdeveloped sense of guilt and responsibility for their happiness. John certainly did. But in his need to keep his parents happy, John was willing to sacrifice the well-being of someone else—his wife.

YOUR CHILD IS MY CHILD

One of the most interesting examples of an invasive, engulfing in-law was told to me by a young colleague of mine named Jill, who called me one day to ask for some advice.

"I can be really strong for my clients, but when it comes to my own life, it's often a whole different story. You know, we've got this baby coming in a few months, and my mother-in-law Evelyn's behavior is bordering on weird. I don't know what to do about it. From the time she found out I was pregnant, she's been referring to the baby as *hers!* 'How's my baby doing? Is my baby kicking a lot today?' Then she goes into great detail about the 'mother/daughter' things she and the baby will be doing together, while making it clear there's no place for me in her fantasy. She's been divorced for a long time and she doesn't seem to have too many friends, so, I guess, she's living vicariously through us. I swear to you, Susan, there are times I've considered leaving Sean just to get away from this woman. I feel so trapped by her constant presence in my life."

I asked Jill what Sean was doing about all this, and got the expected answer:

"Sean knows his mother's behavior is inappropriate, but he's afraid to say anything because (at this point I spoke in unison with Jill) *he doesn't want to hurt her feelings.* But each day that goes by when he doesn't talk to her about this really strains our marriage."

By not dealing directly with his mother's possessiveness, Sean was reinforcing her fantasy and undermining his wife's position and authority. I suggested to Jill that she sit down with Sean, and together they could work out some strategies to nip this nonsense in the bud. Here are the main points that she and Sean needed to address—and if Sean wasn't willing to go along, I told Jill she could do it on her own:

1. Tell Evelyn that you appreciate her excitement about the baby, but there can't be any confusion as to who has what role.
2. Tell Evelyn that from here on out, she needs to find an appropriate term for referring to the baby. "My grandchild," or "my grandbaby," or any term of endearment she likes, as long as it clearly defines who is mother and who is grandmother.

3. Clarify now what she would like the baby to call her. Grandma, or nana, are the two most commonly used terms, but there are plenty of others.
4. Clarify now what her level of participation in your child's life will be. That level should be comfortable for you and your partner, but assure her she will be included as much as possible.

If her nose is a little out of joint at first, don't worry about it. In time she will come to accept your ground rules, and you'll feel a lot less stressed.

Jill was lucky to be able to establish the ground rules ahead of time, because it'll always be more difficult during the tumult that occurs once a new baby arrives. But it's never too late. This clarification is vital, and can be used with any prospective or current grandparent (even if your child or children are older) who is attempting to usurp your role, even though they may be totally oblivious to what they're doing.

DIVIDING TO CONQUER

Sometimes, if your in-laws are not getting the results they want from their own children, they may try to pull you into the fray, another engulfer tactic.

Brad, a soft-spoken thirty-seven-year-old sales rep, had been seeing me for a few weeks because of growing tension between himself and his wife, whom he described as very emotional and hypersensitive. When I asked him what he thought the main source of their current troubles was, he immediately pinpointed his father-in-law, Doug, whom he described as a very intrusive presence in his marriage, even though he lives in another state.

"Jan has been estranged from her father for fifteen years. I met the guy once and he seemed OK—a little rough around the edges, but Jan wants no part of him. Doug has been bombarding her with letters and phone calls for years, using quotes from the Bible to convince Jan that she should 'honor' him as her father and open her heart to him. When he could see he wasn't getting anywhere with her, he switched over to me. He's started writing to me now. Here—I brought a copy of a letter I just got from him that started all this."

I had Brad read the letter aloud to me:

"Dear Brad:

"I am taking the liberty of writing to you in a last-ditch attempt to heal the rift between Jan and myself. As you know, Jan has never forgiven me for the fact that my marriage to her mother was so stormy. I did everything I could to make that marriage work, but I couldn't fight both my wife and her father's money. Jan's grandfather always hated me, and in the end he won out. Both he and Jan's mother have told terrible lies about me, which Jan has bought into.

"I know you love Jan as I do, and I'm sure you can see how the hostility she has for me is hurting her. I know she's struggled with depression and has been seeing a therapist. I hope you don't think I'm being corny when I say that I truly believe her depression would lift if she would just face reality and acknowledge that her mother and grandfather are the reason her childhood was so difficult—not me.

"I think she's been caught up in this rage of hers for so long that it's become second nature. We have to protect her, you and I, because we're the ones who know her best. We both know how much better she would feel if she would just let me back into her life. I'm counting on you to make this happen—don't let me down . . . "

Brad admitted that he was pretty impressed with the intensity of Doug's letter and asked if I didn't think it would be helpful for Jan to have some kind of relationship with her father.

If you were to read Doug's letter without additional information, you would probably be moved by it as Brad was. Here's this poor father just asking for a chance to see his daughter and his grandchildren. OK, so he made some mistakes, but he sounds so convincing and sincere in his concern for his daughter's well-being. Why not try again? After all, what's more important than family?

GETTING THE ALLEGIANCES STRAIGHT

As you've seen throughout this chapter, engulfers normally manipulate their own children to give up big chunks of their lives to them, and it's usually the partner who is chafing against their in-laws' tactics. But Brad and Jan's situation was intriguing because exactly the opposite was happening. I asked Brad to bring Jan in as soon as possible. I had a strong hunch there was a lot more going on in this long-distance invasion than Brad knew.

Jan was quite guarded when she first came in. She acknowledged she was feeling somewhat betrayed by Brad. I sensed that she thought I was also going to push her to reestablish contact with her father in the name of "family" or "forgiveness." I assured her I had no such agenda and really wanted to hear her story, and, even more importantly, I wanted Brad to understand why he needed to support her in whatever decision she made regarding her father. At that point, she relaxed considerably. She began her story in a soft but firm voice.

"My father is totally obsessed with getting back in my life, even though he's remarried and has two other children. But what Brad doesn't understand is that all he really wants is a dumping place for his rage against my mother. He wants me to acknowledge that my mother—who I love—was at fault for everything that went wrong in their marriage, and my grandfather bribed her with a lot of money to leave my father. Now that I'm older and have children of my own, he's convinced that I'll come to my senses. All this happened over twenty years ago, and he can't let go of it. He calls other family members regularly and pleads with them to intervene on his behalf. He's even called childhood friends of mine to remind me what a great father he was. I've started to send his letters back unopened, but just seeing his handwriting can ruin the day for me. Now he's trying to work on my husband. It's like there's this dark presence in my life that I can't get rid of."

I asked Jan if she'd had any face-to-face contact with her father since the estrangement.

"I weakened a few times in the past and met him for dinner, and I've lived to regret it. He never stopped talking about my mother and grandfather and didn't hear a word I said. I felt like I'd been run over by a truck. It's all completely crazy and distorted, but my father has always had his own paranoid version of reality—and he's welcome to it. He was a terrible bully and verbally abusive to me, which he denies, and I don't want him in my life—he has nothing positive to offer me. Why can't he just leave me alone? Brad just can't understand this, because he's got pretty nice parents."

Clearly, Doug wanted a lot more than to have some contact with his daughter. He had an all-consuming need for her to see the reality through his eyes and agree with him that people she loves are malevolent. It was this obsession that initially drove the wedge between Jan and Doug, whom she described as "rageful" and a "control freak."

Through his incessant, unwanted efforts to get back into Jan's life, and his harangues about her mother, Doug was continuing to bully and abuse her. He took absolutely no responsibility for his own behavior and projected the blame for his earlier divorce on everyone else. He even denied that he had been abusive. But now his weapons were written words instead of the high-volume tirades Jan told me he unleashed on her regularly when she was little.

I asked Jan how much of this she had told Brad.

"Probably very little—I've just told him that I don't want to see my father, and I wanted him to stop nagging me about it. But it's difficult to go into all this ugliness and in a sense have to relive it. . . ."

"So how," I asked her gently, "could he have understood the whole picture and give you the validation you want when he only had a few sketchy outlines?"

I looked over at Brad who was visibly shaken. And then he really came through. "I'm so sorry, Jan," he said. "I'll handle this. I'll let him know in no uncertain terms that he is to stop harassing you and we'll use every legal means at our disposal if he doesn't."

Engulfers, like all manipulators, often play divide and conquer. But Jan had somehow expected Brad to read her mind and somehow be able to see the whole picture without much information.

Without her personal story, Brad didn't know what it was she needed from him, and Jan was reluctant to tell him. Instead, she got tense and resentful. But once everything was out on the table, Doug's attempts to enlist Brad as his ally didn't work. Instead, Jan got the ally she needed.

FROM CRISIS TO ENGULFMENT

Few things can activate as intense an ethical and moral dilemma for your partner as a crisis in a parent's life. We all respond viscerally to the news that a parent is ill, or has suffered a loss, or is struggling—and it's natural to be pulled in at such a time. What's not natural, or healthy, are parents' expectations that their crisis entitles them to take over their adult child's life long after they are able to help themselves. It's at that point that crisis slips into engulfment.

Julia, a pale, tense middle-aged woman with bitten-off nails and about forty extra pounds on her small frame, told me that she'd called me because her husband had threatened to leave her unless she talked to a therapist about her engulfing mother.

"It's been hell since my father died a year and a half ago. My mother was so depressed, we all worried about her. She wouldn't eat, couldn't sleep by herself, so my sisters and I took turns looking in on her and helping her with all the financial and legal stuff that was so overwhelming to her. Al was OK with it for a while, but as time went on, Mom started saying I was the only one she trusted to look out for her best interests. She picked fights with my sisters, and then she wanted more and more time from me. It's been more than a year, and I'm still over there almost every day. My sisters tell me I'm nuts—Mom can afford to hire lawyers, and accountants, and someone to take care of the house—but I feel like she did everything for me for years of my life, and family should take care of family. It's just that I'm falling apart, Susan. My husband hates me, my kids feel abandoned, and even Mom thinks I'm not spending enough time with her. The only thing that makes me feel remotely better is food."

Julia's husband, Al, a short, curly-haired insurance broker, was happy to come in for a joint session. He was visibly nervous and upset.

"I don't understand how Molly went from being a woman who was smart and vivacious to this person who behaves like she'll fall apart if Julia's not over there every day helping her pay her bills or cook dinner. Yes, she lost her husband. And I'm trying to be compassionate. I know it was terrible for her, and I'm not diminishing that. But it didn't kill her brain cells. She's the same person. But now she's trained Julia to fetch and roll over for her, and, of course, she doesn't want to give that up. We've hired people to come in and she fires them. She's using us, and Julia refuses to see it."

I asked Al to tell me what all this uproar was doing to him and to his and Julia's marriage.

"Julia looks at me like I'm a serial killer when I say that it's time for her to let her mom stand on her own two feet, but I'm at the point where I'm ready to grab the phone out of Julia's hand and yell, 'No, Julia's not coming over, dammit!' Come on. It's getting—no it's gotten—ridiculous. Our whole life is changed—all the things we love doing together have been put on hold because 'someone's got to look after Mom.' Well, it's been a year and a half. And Mom still refuses to see a doctor and get help with her depression. She refuses to join any of the activities we've suggested to her. She insists that she'll die without Julia."

At that point, Al broke into tears. "I don't have a wife, a lover, a companion, a friend, any more—it's tearing me up."

Al was absolutely right when he said it was time for Molly to stand on her own two feet. There was nothing callous or uncaring about his position. Molly was physically well, had enough money to hire a companion or live-in help, and could start to build a new life for herself as millions of widowed people have done. But Molly's refusal to get treatment for her depression and her insistence that nobody could take care of her except Julia appeared to provide her with some semblance of control. Molly needed professional help, and no family member can provide that.

I wondered why Julia wasn't able to set some limits with her mother. Her answer was hardly surprising:

"I just feel so guilty when I tell her I can't come over or suggest she look up some old friends. So I just do what she wants—I can't stand to make her any more unhappy than she already is. But I know I can't go on like this—that's why we're here. I'd be grateful for any suggestions you can give us."

A family crisis can quickly slip into engulfment when your in-laws send a clear SOS to your partner that he or she is all that stands between them and despair or ill health, even death.

I certainly wasn't suggesting that Julia and Al shouldn't be loving and supportive. But more often than not, becoming the sole caretaker or companion may, as was clear in Julia's case, actually impede the needy parent's ability to get either physically or emotionally stronger. It will certainly shake up even the most solid marriage.

Later in this book, you will see how Julia and Al were able to reclaim their life together and at the same time find a wonderful solution to helping Molly out of the pit she had sunken into. I will also give you some practical and effective methods for helping a genuinely incapacitated parent who cannot live without assistance.

A TIGHTENING GRIP

Engulfers can twist the bonds of love into a tight leash, sometimes pulling your partner and you so close you have no room to move. They need your partner and, by extension, you. They want you. Their life isn't complete or good without you. They make unreasonable demands on your time and attention, though those demands may come in sparkling, gift-wrapped boxes or draped with endearments. At their darkest, engulfing in-laws ignore even the clearest requests for change or restrictions on their behavior. They invade your routines with manipulation and exaggerated assumptions about their role in your life. And if you let them, they grip you so tightly that they may also squeeze the life out of your marriage.

4

The Controllers

"They can't let us live our own lives."

"They won't mind their own business."

"Why can't they treat us like adults?"

Welcome to the not-so-wonderful world of the controllers.

In the family structure they created long before you arrived on the scene, controllers hold the ultimate authority, and they have no intention of giving it up. They're top dogs who need inferiors to maintain their status, and that means their adult children are expected to be permanent dependents. Equality and independence, the natural, desirable touchstones we all strive for, are not part of the controllers' plan. In large ways and small, they let your partner know that he or she lacks the character and resources to survive outside their orbit. The critics you saw in the previous chapter try to make you feel inferior, but the primary target of controllers is your partner, their child. The underlying message is always "You're selfish, you'll fail, you can't and don't deserve to make it on your own," the natural extension being "so let me run your life for you."

The controllers' agenda may sound pretty severe, but most, or at least many, of them aren't calculatedly plotting how to make your life miserable. They do, however, want the sense of order, satisfaction, and superiority that comes from towering above their children—it's what feels right to them. When something tips the balance of power away from them, they almost automatically do whatever it takes to put themselves back at the helm—overt threats; angry scenes; withdrawal of love, money, and approval; as well as more subtle manipulations and guilt-peddling. It's easy for them to select the tactic that will elicit the fastest results. After all, controlling in-laws were almost always controlling parents, so they've had a long time to practice.

THE WEDDING BELL IS THEIR STARTING BELL

One of the first occasions on which controllers will test their ability to shape your decisions in a way that pleases them will most likely be the big day—your wedding.

Sarah, a tall, red-haired thirty-one-year-old medical assistant, came to see me because, as she put it, "I've had it and I want you to tell me if this marriage can be salvaged."

Sarah told me that she'd been locked in a power struggle with her mother-in-law from the very beginning, when she and her accountant husband, Devon, realized that their ideas about their wedding didn't match what Devon's mother, Claire, had in mind.

"We were both working long hours, and his parents were

going through a really rancorous divorce. My parents live in Europe, and it would have been 'so who should we invite,' and we decided that what we really wanted was a very quiet, very private ceremony with just immediate family and about half a dozen friends. Claire took our decision about the wedding as a personal affront. She lives in Colorado, so she would bombard us with phone calls—actually, she was harder on Devon than on me, and he's not at all good in dealing with her, which, of course, frustrates the hell out of me. She would say things to him like 'How can you turn what should be the happiest day of my life into a slap in the face? What am I supposed to tell the rest of the family? Are you ashamed of us? You're just trying to ruin this for everyone.' Then she told Devon that he was the same screw-up he'd always been, and he would regret this for the rest of his life. She even went so far as to have their minister call Devon to tell him how much pain he was causing his mother and how much it would mean to Claire for us to have a 'real' wedding. And, of course, he reminded us of how generous she was being by offering to pay for everything. Didn't she have any idea how much she was spoiling things for us?"

Typically for a controller, Claire was far more concerned with what she wanted than with what anyone else wanted, and Sarah was understandably upset and bewildered by the lengths her prospective mother-in-law would go to to get her own way. Those early clashes also planted worrisome seeds in Sarah's mind. As she saw how Claire's attacks affected Devon, she became increasingly concerned about how well her partner could protect her.

"All this was really hard on Devon. He was really anxious and I could see him beginning to doubt himself. He started saying things like 'Are you sure we won't regret skipping the big party?' As if he hadn't told me he'd never wanted anything big and fancy. I can't believe how Claire hounded him. I know she was having a rough time in her own life and I came along when she was really leaning on Devon. He and I are really close, and I suffered for how much garbage he was going through. He would jump every time the phone rang. He got very withdrawn, knowing he was going to have to deal with her anger, which, I think, still scares him. That kind of tension was really hard on our relationship. Several times he would falter and say we should just give her 'the kind of wedding she wants.' It took a lot of strength to hold my ground. I reminded him that Claire had *her* wedding—this was *our* wedding, in case he hadn't noticed. But he just couldn't say to her, 'This is what we need to do for us.' "

Claire was going through a difficult divorce and undoubtedly feeling frightened and off-balance. If she could get Devon to give in once more and agree to a big wedding, she could temporarily postpone having to deal with Devon's lessening need of her and continue to feel involved in his life. She was entitled to be disappointed at Devon and Sarah's plans, and to express that disappointment directly. But she had no right to wage a relentless campaign to try to wear them down and commandeer their plans.

For her part, Sarah believed Devon should be able to take a firm stand with his mother. The only problem was that Devon and Claire had long ago perfected their dance of control and capitulation. Claire believed Devon would give in to her as he had so often in the past, and he would do anything to avoid confronting her attacks. The harsh reality is that it was unrealistic for Sarah to think Devon could short-circuit the training of a lifetime and easily take on his mother.

Even though Devon and Sarah went ahead with their plans and had the wedding they wanted, Devon felt a lot of remorse about what he did. Never forget: If you have controlling in-laws, your partner pays a significant emotional price to be loyal to you.

CONTROL KNOWS NO GENDER

The stereotype of the controlling, interfering mother-in-law has been the staple of comedians, talk-shows, advice columns, and the popular comic strip *Momma* for a long time. But mothers-in-law have no monopoly on bullying, manipulation, or guilt-peddling when they want their way.

David, an amiable twenty-seven-year-old musician who plays clarinet in a local symphony orchestra, was clearly agitated as he told me about the pressure his father-in-law, Norm, a successful anesthesiologist, had been putting on Shelley, an associate in a large law firm. As with Sarah and Devon, the pressure emerged, loud and clear, when it came time to plan the wedding.

"Shelley's parents are practicing Catholics, but Shelley hasn't been to church in years and she's very interested in some of the Eastern religions. I'm from a long line of non-observant Jews. We agreed that since neither of us is into organized religion all that much, we'd expose our kids to a lot of different ideas—to us the best religion is being a good person. We wanted to get married in this really great little hotel by the ocean, but Norm had other ideas. We ended up getting married in a church, because he made such a stink, and I went along, because I didn't want to start out being the bad guy, which made me feel like a total wimp, especially since my own parents' feelings were totally ignored."

As David found out, your father-in-law may be the real control expert in your new family. Norm worked on Shelley, arguing that since she didn't care about religion, she should at least give him the peace and pleasure of knowing she'd had a Catholic wedding. He knew that he could count on Shelley to pressure David to change their plans.

Controlling in-laws regularly attempt to steer and override your decisions about your life choices. Sometimes, the issue is not major, and you can go along with what your in-law wants without any great harm. However, in David's situation, capitulation about something as important as his religious preferences really violated his core beliefs and personal integrity.

Controlling in-laws like Claire and Norm have very definite ideas about how your life should unfold, and when those ideas clash with yours, the wedding becomes a powerful, symbolic challenge to their authority. As a result, all too many weddings have been turned into a war zone fraught with tension and resentments that will inevitably play out between you and your partner. And as David found out, there can be a lot more at stake than which florist or caterer to use.

A CONTINUING CAMPAIGN

Once he had successfully gotten his daughter and son-in-law to change their wedding arrangements, Norm was all set to intensify his control tactics.

When David and Shelley had their first child, Norm made the baby the focus of his campaign to force his values and beliefs on them. David reached the boiling point when Norm started lobbying Shelley to have the new baby baptized.

"He's been hounding Shelley ever since she got pregnant. First, he wanted her to use an obstetrician friend of his that Shelley doesn't like. Then he wanted us to name the baby after his late brother. . . . But all that pales in comparison to the pressure he's putting on us about the baptism. He grinds Shelley down by reminding her of how close they've always been, and how much he's done for her, and how she didn't want to go to an Ivy League school but it got her where she is today. He keeps telling her how young she is, and that she mustn't make impulsive decisions she'll regret later. After all, he's older and has had much more life experience and all that crap. . . . When she dares to disagree with him, he really loses it and starts screaming that she's an ingrate and just maybe he'll have to make some changes in his will. He can't stand to see her make any decisions of her own. I think he'd breathe for her if he could."

It's maddening to see a controlling in-law's repetitive efforts to keep your partner from growing up. With words and behavior, Norm was feeding Shelley the steady message that while she might be a married woman and an effective professional, she was somehow incapable of making sound decisions about almost anything—especially if those decisions clashed with what he wanted. Her father's jibes about her adequacy, combined with his anger and veiled threats, were enough to force Shelley to take the easy way out:

"Now she's saying she doesn't care that much—let's get Steven baptized and make her father happy—and it's causing a real rift between us. Nobody gives a damn about what I feel or believe. I thought she and I were clear about how we wanted to raise our kids. This time, I'm not backing down! How can she just toss something this important aside because she can't stand to say no to her father?"

To David, as the newcomer, the issues seemed relatively simple. You just tell Norm something like "I respect your beliefs and I would appreciate it if you would do the same with us. I know it's difficult for you, but you're just going to have to accept that we're going to raise our child the way we think is best." And with a different kind of father-in-law and a different kind of partner, that would have established some appropriate boundaries. There might have been some discussion, some adult-to-adult airing of disappointments and resentments, but, ultimately, the subject would be closed. Not so, however, with a controlling parent and a still-compliant child. Even with the squabbles over the wedding, David hadn't fully realized just how much power Norm had over Shelley until the conflict over the baptism came up. He was incredulous at how Shelley could be so different with her family than she was with everyone else.

"Here's this incredible woman that I not only love but really respect and admire. I've heard her on the phone with her boss and she really can stand up for herself and deal very effectively with almost everybody, including me. But she turns to Jell-O when it comes to any kind of conflict with her father."

David had met and fallen in love with the Shelley who was mature and confident, and it bewildered him that she left her assertiveness outside the front door when she had to deal with her father. Like many children of controlling parents, Shelley functioned just fine in the outside world, where relationships are not weighed down with years' worth of expectations, demands, and judgments as they are with parents. But she had never developed a separate identity when it came to her parents, especially her father. Caught between conflicting loyalties to her father and her husband, Shelley often chose the person she had the longer history with, even though it was putting a significant strain on her marriage. As you will see throughout this chapter, upsetting the new member of the family is often less frightening and guilt-laden than taking on the controlling parent.

From the information David gave me, it was obvious that Norm wasn't going to let Shelley make her own decisions and be her own person without putting up one hell of a battle first. Noncontrolling in-laws are able to:

- Openly discuss conflicts with you and your partner
- Negotiate or barter
- Work toward some resolution where nobody has to win or lose

But Norm couldn't do that. When his daughter married, he believed that he suffered a catastrophic loss of status and role-identity. And when people lose something, they struggle desperately to get it back.

If Norm could shake Shelley's confidence in her perceptions and her sense of herself as a grown woman, keeping her cut off from her strength and intellect, maybe he could get her to lean on and obey him just a little longer. Then he could feel more powerful, more needed.

SHOWING WHO'S BOSS

I've always found it interesting that so many controllers manage to have their children or their children's partner working in the family business. That leaves the door open for them to exert control not only over your personal life, but your livelihood as well. Even in the best of situations, there are inherent risks in working in a parent's or in-law's business. The power balance is very skewed, and despite the financial benefits or seeming security that may come your way, the price you ultimately pay can be extremely dear.

Mara is a twenty-seven-year-old dancer with a long black ponytail. Her new husband, Rob, works with his father, Jack, and one of his uncles in the family accounting firm. Mara told me that Jack constantly berates Rob in front of other people, and seems to love making him feel insecure. Rob has been promised that the firm will be his in the future, but Mara is far more concerned about the present. She came to see me, distraught and angry about how Jack managed to stand in the way of a trip to Europe she and Rob had been planning for more than a year:

"I don't know if our marriage can survive if things continue like this. Rob lives in constant fear of failing his father. A week before we were ready to leave on our trip, Jack tells us we can't go. He tells Rob, 'I can't believe you would even think of taking off at a time like this. You know one of our most important clients is having an audit, and you're way behind with the record-keeping, as usual.' When Rob balked, his father said, 'Be a grown-up for once in your life! You owe me—your place is here—not running around Europe like an idiot, wasting your money.' This is total bullshit! First of all, it's just a routine audit, and both his father and uncle can deal with it. And second, they knew we had all our tickets and reservations. But Rob didn't even get mad. He said he couldn't have a good time knowing his father was upset, so, of course, we've canceled everything. First I was devastated, but now I'm furious. What kind of man did I marry? If this is the way things are going to be, I don't want any part of it!"

Jack's timing was certainly interesting. And even more interesting was the question of why Rob continued in a job where he was treated like the village idiot, and which was tearing his marriage apart to boot. Sure, he might own the business some day, but what would be left of his self-respect by the time he did? The hope that was pulling him along was almost certainly unrealistic. When controllers put carrots on the end of a stick to make an untenable situation seem bearable, they're highly likely to snatch the prize away when you go to claim it. I've seen many people promise a family member the moon in exchange for obedience. But years later, when the controller either retires or dies, the adult child is devastated to discover that the reward is not there. They have not been given or left what they were promised. Their only true legacy is a deeply eroded sense of emotional well-being from years of permitting themselves to be mistreated.

Mara said she was sick of seeing her husband belittled and pushed around. I asked her what she was doing with all her anger. She hesitated for a few moments and then hid her face as if she were deeply ashamed.

"I'm dumping it on him, of course. I'm telling him he's weak and neurotic. And . . . I'm drinking . . . which really scares me. My father's an alcoholic and I vowed I would never be like him. I feel so alone—Rob works such long hours and when he gets home he's usually exhausted. . . . We haven't made love for weeks . . . "

RIGHT PROBLEM, WRONG SOLUTION

A marriage affected by controlling in-laws is guaranteed to be a breeding ground for anger, resentment, and, often, contempt. You are filled with resentment at the people who seem to have all the power. They're pulling the strings and won't leave you alone to live your own life. And, like Mara, you may be increasingly incensed at your partner's inability to pull away from an obviously unhealthy situation or even to protect you from it. And if that's not enough to flatten a marriage, you can throw in your partner's anger at you for nagging him about a problem he already feels ashamed about. It can feel overwhelming and hopeless. No wonder so many targets of controlling in-laws are ready to throw in the towel.

I asked Mara to raise her head and look at me. I told her she was understandably very angry about how much she and Rob were under her very demanding father-in-law's control. I knew that she had no idea what she could do to make the situation better. Instead, she was descending into depression, drinking, and rage—behaviors that resolved nothing and were guaranteed to make the situation worse, strengthening Jack's position. Together, we would find far better ways to deal with her frustrations and get her marriage onto a healthier plane.

THEIR MONEY AND YOUR LIFE

With controllers, money and approval are strongly linked. They often give and withhold their resources in response to your choices, making a tangible commentary on how well you're pleasing them. As you saw with Mara and Rob, they may promise great financial rewards when you and your partner do what they want you to do.

Sarah's mother-in-law, Claire, used money as a way of trying to re-create a family structure that no longer existed:

"Devon's mother manipulates him totally—not just with guilt, but with money. She takes what she knows is a problem for us—money—and eliminates all the reasons we can't come and see her. She'll buy the plane tickets, so then we feel we have no choice. She's very generous, but there are always strings—no, ropes—attached. Now she's offering to buy us a house, but only if it's in Colorado, where she lives. She keeps saying things like 'Wouldn't it be nice to build your dream house here? Wouldn't it be nice if we could all live in the same city? I saw a lovely lot the other day that would be perfect for you.' Well, we don't want to live in Colorado. Our life is here, in Los Angeles. Devon asked her if she would give or lend us the money to buy a house in California and she said no, because California real estate is too overpriced."

Claire's message was clear: Do it my way, and you'll get the money. Do it your way, and you won't. Claire's attempts at control through money were certainly more benign than Jack's, but she, too, was trying to turn the purse strings into an umbilical cord.

UPPING THE ANTE

When some controllers see that they're not getting their way, they will alternate promises of financial goodies with threats of disinheritance or financial punishments if your partner doesn't toe the line.

Stephanie, a forty-five-year-old copy editor for a local television news program, came into her marriage to Andy, a tall, outgoing cameraman at the same station, with what her in-laws considered to be unacceptable baggage. Stephanie had been married and divorced twice, and a wife with that history was certainly not what Andy's parents had in mind for their son.

Andy described his parents as extremely rigid, and said they were beside themselves when he announced he was going to marry Stephanie, doing everything they could to dissuade him. As Stephanie told me:

"They really went nuts before the wedding. Andy was spending a lot of time at my place, and they would call three or four times a night to check up on him. When they saw they couldn't change his mind, they told him that if he married me, he was no longer a member of the family and they were cutting him out of their will. And, of course, they reminded him of how much money *that* meant. For a while he really couldn't handle the pressure, so we kept breaking up and getting back together again. Finally, I told him that I couldn't marry someone who let his parents control him so totally."

And Andy added:

"I had no idea if they meant it about the will, and, quite honestly, I didn't care about the money so much, but I knew they would have to be pretty upset to make a threat like that, and I did care about upsetting them to this extent. I knew we were in for some major problems with them, but I was so crazy about this woman, nothing was going to stop me from marrying her. I made some attempts to make everybody happy. I tried to reassure my parents they would come to love Stephanie. I tried to reassure Stephanie things would get better, even though I didn't really believe that myself."

Threats of grim financial consequences if you cross them are a big part of the controllers' heavy artillery. How many times have you or someone you know heard things like "If you marry that person, you're out of my will," or "If you don't go to medical school, I'm cutting you off financially"? In Andy's case, his parents felt they were losing control over their son's life and destiny because he was marrying a woman they saw as morally inferior. If he was going to defy them, they would retaliate and, hopefully, bring enough pressure to bear to get him to give her up.

I told Andy that I had no way of predicting if his father would make good on his threats. I have seen parents do what they've threatened to do, and others who are just trying to bully you and ultimately back down. But it really didn't matter. What kind of future disasters would Andy be setting himself up for if he allowed his father to control his choice of a wife?

Money is much more than currency or a means of buying things. It has a powerful symbolic relationship to love, trust, competence, approval, and, of course, power. As a result, even if you have ample resources of your own, you can expect many controlling in-laws to pull out the promise of money—and use it to exert their will over you and your partner.

CONTROL THROUGH GUILT AND INTIMIDATION

Tommy managed to slip off his parents' leash long enough to marry Leslie, but that seemed to take all the will he had. As time went on, he reverted to letting his parents call the shots.

"His mother called him up on his twenty-fifth birthday, crying. 'You're our only son. It's your birthday, we want to see you.' And then they added, 'Just you.' Then his father got on the phone and told him he was an ingrate who disrespected his mother, and to get the hell over there. So Tommy said he had to be with his parents, even though we had made plans for the evening and he felt terrible about changing them. So he went. And I cried myself to sleep."

Tommy's parents used methods of control that were not only ridiculous but insulting. But what in the world was going on with Tommy? Yes, he was very young, and yes, this was his first time living away from his parents, but he was behaving like a puppet on a string. They were still running his life, and he seemed to have no clue as to even the most basic emotional meaning of being married.

AN OLD, FAMILIAR SCRIPT

This family melodrama didn't start when Tommy met Leslie. It had been going on since Tommy was little. Seeing his mother fall into depression when he was away from her, then cheer up when he was close, had left him with the feeling that it was his job to keep his mother afloat. And, of course, if he didn't, his father, the controller, would step in and demand it. So Tommy often gave up activities and friends to be with the family and dutifully joined the family business as soon as he graduated high school. He had dreamed of going on to college and becoming a police officer, but he turned his back on those plans because his mother didn't want to let him out of her sight, and his father cruelly suggested that he couldn't make it on his own.

As an adult, Tommy wasn't emotionally evolved enough to realize that he needed to transfer his primary loyalty to his wife. In fact, as we've seen with so many children of controlling parents, shifting his priorities would have created unbearable guilt and deep feelings of betrayal within him. So he continued to do what he'd always done—jump when his parents whistled. And his familiar patterns of always giving in and catering to his parents' demands soon relegated his wife to the background.

THE BELIEFS THAT BIND

As for Leslie, she's not a passive person, and yet she had let herself become embroiled in a family drama that sounded like theater of the absurd. I asked her if she ever tried to do something about what was obviously turning into an intolerable situation.

"I told Tommy this has got to stop, but he was this barrier between them and me. So I felt I couldn't say anything. I know I should have run, I know most people don't live like this, but I was very young, and I was in love, he was making good money working for his folks, and I couldn't believe it wouldn't get better."

When I saw Tommy and Leslie together the first time, a lot of things fell into place. Would Tommy rather upset

Leslie than his parents? In a word, yes. For him, as with so many of the people in this book, it was unthinkable to take on the giants, even when it caused both him and his partner tremendous pain. For years, he told me, he'd taken orders from his father, who'd always taken pains to point out how much Tommy let his mother down when she needed him, and was quick to criticize his every mistake. Remember, controllers control by making others feel inadequate, and they're quick to remember failures—a broad category that includes practically anything not aligned with their preferences.

Tommy had taken all of this in, and a big part of him still believed that his parents held the key to his emotional survival. So it only followed that upsetting or displeasing them would be catastrophic for him. His only recourse, he believed, was to hand his life over to them.

HOPE VERSUS HABITS

I told Leslie that she'd been waiting for five years for her love, logic, or anger to miraculously turn Tommy into her advocate, and it didn't look as if that was going to happen any time soon. It's never easy to disconnect the hopes, fears, and blind loyalties that are consciously or unconsciously leading to your partner's compliance. Your in-laws are the people who wired your partner's original set of hot buttons, and your partner's reactions to them are often neither rational nor logical, but driven by unconscious conflicts and impulsive reactions.

But before Leslie decided to give up on Tommy, I assured her none of this meant that, with both of our efforts, Tommy couldn't make some changes. And certainly there were many changes she could make in the way she was handling the situation, that could—and did—turn things around dramatically.

ENTER THE GRANDCHILDREN

If you thought your in-laws were controlling before, just wait until you have children. The critics may shake their heads and cluck their tongues as they witness your parenting abilities, but controlling in-laws go one step further—they actually try to undermine your authority as parents.

Having competed with you for your partner's loyalty, once they become grandparents, they put themselves in direct competition with both you and your partner for your children's attention and affection. It would be impossible to describe every scenario I've come across in which this type of undermining occurs, but it's common for them to ignore the rules, routines, and methods of discipline you've put in place for your children and substitute their own. They may try to influence which school your kids attend and what kind of religious upbringing they should have, and they may become involved at the level of what they should eat and when to toilet-train them. If you have in-laws who use your children as a means of validating their own worth and superiority, you know how infuriating this particular manifestation of control can be.

In chapter 2, you met Karen and Cal. You saw how Karen's father, Ray, rarely missed an opportunity to belittle his son-in-law in the name of helping him out. Karen had always been quick to defend Ray, which made Cal feel pretty resentful. But Cal told me of an episode that had finally changed Karen's perceptions about her father's motives:

"Our son, Derek, is eight, and he was dying for a certain video game. We said fine, but he'd have to earn it, since we'd just gotten him a new bike for his birthday. We set up some extra responsibilities for him around the house and agreed to pay him for them. We told him, as soon as he earned half of what he needed, we'd match it, and he could get his game. He was ecstatic. But then Grandpa takes him to a ball game one day, and he comes back with the video game! Now, we had told my in-laws about the deal we had with Derek, but, once again, Ray set it up so that I looked bad and he could be the hero. Ray and Derek against the mean parents."

Of course, there's nothing wrong with indulging a child from time to time. If this had been the first time Ray had gone against Karen and Cal's wishes, it probably wouldn't have been that big a deal, but it was part of a pattern of undermining that began between Ray and Cal even before Derek was born. Fortunately, something positive did come out of this minidrama:

"Believe it or not, Karen was really pissed at her dad. We told Derek we'd put the toy away until he'd met his part of the bargain, and all hell broke loose. Finally, Karen told her father that while she didn't want to deprive him of a relationship with Derek, he couldn't do this again—he was overstepping his boundaries. God, I wish she'd been able to take a firm stand with him earlier, but better late than never. At least, now we're on the same team."

Ray had shown earlier, when Cal was building the office for Karen, just how competitive he was, making sure everyone knew he was the expert. It's hard for a powerful parent figure to relinquish even a little of that role, and when you start a family of your own, it's infuriating to have a grandparent ride roughshod over your wishes and rules. And it's hard for you not to come across like the heavy when you're trying to hold the line and your in-laws are looking generous and giving.

Ray could have avoided all the friction if he had talked the situation over with his daughter and son-in-law and asked them if it would be all right for him to buy the game for

Derek. But Ray was very manipulative, and manipulators are rarely direct. So instead of negotiating, he created an unnecessary power struggle that put poor Derek in the middle, made Ray look like the good guy, and ended up upsetting everyone.

CONTROLLERS ARE CRIPPLERS

Controllers may have some wonderful traits, and their need to control may not define the entire relationship with them. But no matter how positive or supportive they may sometimes be, if they're out to run your life and impose their will on you, and your partner has never been able to stand up to them, all the good things they do won't offset how enraged and powerless they can make you feel.

Healthy parents build their children's sense of self-worth, preparing them to leave home emotionally as well as physically. But toxic, controlling in-laws are less concerned with what's best for their children than they are with what feels comfortable to them. They will do whatever they think necessary, including crippling your partner's sense of confidence and independence, to maintain the precarious but familiar power structure in which you and your partner are at the bottom of the heap. They desperately want to stay in control, even if that means wrecking your marriage.

It's as if they are saying: "I will intimidate you, invade your life, load you up with guilt, and strip you of your confidence so I can keep control over you to show you how much I love you." Obviously, their behavior has little to do with love.

5

The Masters of Chaos

The toxic in-laws we've met so far have been active and aggressive in putting their stamp on your marriage. They pressure you and your partner to mold your life into the shape that they want, and whatever tactics they use, they attempt to assume a dominant, hands-on role in your relationship.

But the people you'll meet in this chapter are different. In fact, they may rarely, if ever, be overly concerned with your marriage at all. These are the in-laws whose own lives are so unhappy and so chaotic that they create a spinning vortex of ever-escalating crises and disasters.

Whether you're dealing with in-laws who are caught in a hostile or raging relationship with each other, substance abusers, those who are sexually inappropriate with you or other family members, financially irresponsible people, or those who abused your partner as a child, these individuals are doing such terrible things to themselves and each other that their actions are impossible to ignore. And as their instability escalates and their lives implode, the stability of your marriage will be inevitably shaken.

Why? Because, as we'll see, chaotic in-laws have an almost magnetic ability to draw your partner into their erratic, unstable orbit.

IN-LAWS WHO LIVE IN THE COMBAT ZONE

Some couples live in a state of hair-trigger volatility. They mistrust each other, have long-standing grudges, and stage window-rattling battles. When you marry into their midst, your life is suddenly set against a backdrop of constant conflict—even when they live far away. They break up and make up, bouncing from crisis to crisis, and in many cases, one or both of them turn to your partner for support. Suddenly, it seems, your partner is hopelessly entangled in their undeclared war—comforting or mediating or listening to endless attacks—and when that happens, your in-laws wind up with as much influence in your life as the most determined controller. It takes an enormous amount of time and energy for you and your partner to build your life together, and battling in-laws who siphon off both of those vital resources are cutting off your marriage at the roots.

Dana, a tall, thirty-year-old graphic artist, came to see me with her husband Mark, a set designer for a successful television series. Throughout the time Dana and Mark have been together, Dana has been caught up in a family drama with her parents, that spins out of control on a regular basis, and Mark is rapidly running out of patience.

"I'm sorry," he began, "but I just don't understand what

my wife thinks she's accomplishing by spending so much time on the phone with her mother and running over there all the time. The last time, it was after midnight, and it was raining hard, and she had an accident—I'm sure it was because she was so upset about her mom. Thank god, she wasn't hurt, but what about the next time? Dana really believes if she just holds Gloria's hand, and supports her, and helps her find a lawyer, this time she'll really go through with a divorce. But her mother is never going to leave—this has been going on for thirty years, and in the seven years I've been on the scene, it's crystal-clear to me that she's always crying wolf. This business of saying "It's all over, I'm walking out" is just something she does. I don't know why Dana can't see it. Her mother loves to piss and moan about how awful Dana's dad is, but she's too scared to do anything about it. So she unloads on Dana, and then she feels better and Dana feels worse. I've had it with her crazy parents, I want them out of our lives, and I know I'm taking my anger out on Dana, and I'm here because I don't know what to do . . . "

SHIFTING THE DISCOMFORT

Mark seemed to have a clear take on what was going on. When he said that Dana feels worse and her mom feels better after Gloria gets through with her venting, he was pinpointing a very common but subtle piece of behavior I call "shifting the discomfort."

Dana's mother has for years been using her daughter as a dumping ground to unload her anger and unhappiness with her husband. By agonizing over her problems to her daughter and making her feel so torn up about them, Gloria has mobilized Dana's rescue fantasies. Dana inevitably becomes so worried about how awful her mother is feeling that she begins to take responsibility for her mother's salvation. And when she does that, Gloria can avoid having to take responsibility for her own life. For Gloria, the dump-on-Dana-and-run strategy almost always works.

For Dana, though, the overwhelming desire to rescue a mother whose life was in perpetual turmoil had become a top priority, eclipsing everything else, including her marriage. She knew that her Super Daughter tendencies were a problem, but she insisted that this time was different. This time the crisis was of a different magnitude.

As Dana explained:

"Things have gotten really bad between my parents lately. This past week they had a terrible fight—my mom is convinced he's seeing another woman—and my father just walked out and moved into a hotel. It's happened before, but this time it sounds like he's really not coming back. My mom's been sobbing to me on the phone—she's such a wreck she hasn't been able to go to work. She's been asking what I think she should do, and telling me about all the awful things he's done. I get very caught up in calling her, counseling her—I even call her from work. I know Mark is really resentful of all the time I talk about her and to her and all the time I go over there. I know he wants me to tell her, 'Please don't involve me,' but how could I live with myself if I did that? It's really a no-brainer—I think she should finally get a divorce. This time, I think she'll do it, so I've been trying to give her all the support I can. She says she gets more out of talking to me than any therapist or counselor."

"Which," I said to Dana, "must make you feel pretty powerful."

"It does," she answered, a little sheepishly. "Ever since I was a kid, my mother's been using me as her confidante, telling me how awful my father was and how unhappy she was. I wanted so much to save her—to make her life better. . . . Imagine—my mom would finally be happy. That seemed like it was worth whatever sacrifice I had to make."

"But nothing ever changed, did it?" I asked.

She was very quiet for a moment and tears came to her eyes:

"No. . . . Nothing ever changed. They'd get back to 'normal,' the big catastrophe would be over, and she would say, 'Just forget all those things I told you.' It was totally embarrassing—I was so ashamed of my bizarre parents. Then I'd get this awful thud in the stomach that she'd done it again—and she'd done it *to me* again!"

Dana was reacting predictably to her mother's latest call for help, just as she had done from the time she was a teenager—with equally frustrating results.

I told her that no child of any age belongs in the middle of two battling parents. There's nothing she could have done about the situation, and it was almost a given that she would always end up feeling helpless and inadequate—and made a fool of. But Dana was running on pure adrenaline, driven much more by emotion than logic, and unaware of the consequences to her own emotional well-being, as well as to her marriage, of becoming so enmeshed in her parents' lives.

THRIVING ON UPROAR

There are many couples like Mark's in-laws. Couples who battle their way through to the end of their lives. They seem to need the high drama and the rush of fighting, slamming doors, exploding, screaming, and acting as if each battle is really it—this time they're through with each other. Then they get back to what is "normal" for them and frequently act as if nothing ever happened, leaving their adult children bewildered, frustrated, and often exhausted from their useless attempts to rescue one or both parents. As Dana described it:

"It's like being on a treadmill that never goes anywhere."

It was clear from the information Dana and Mark gave me that Dana's parents were bonded together through anger and drama. Gloria loved to complain and play the victim of her brutish husband, who, according to Dana, constantly demeaned and verbally abused her. Dana, too, was convinced her father had been seeing other women for several years. But Gloria was either too frightened, or too paralyzed, or too neurotically fused to her husband, Paul, to ever take any steps to make her life better.

And Dana was too consumed by the needs and fantasies of saving her mother, which had been engendered in her from adolescence, to be able to see any options for herself other than to do what she'd always done. When it didn't work, like most people, she just did more of the same, which, of course, upset Mark, who was forced to share his wife with an unhappy and self-defeating mother. With guidance and effort, though, that frustrating cycle would soon change.

"I AM NOT AN ALCOHOLIC"

"That's my father-in-law Vic's mantra," sighed Greg, a smart thirty-three-year-old computer programmer. "Every time there's a family dinner, or a birthday, or a holiday, he starts with the vodka in the afternoon, and by the time the evening rolls around, he's absolutely out of it. He drinks to the point where he becomes silly and infantile. He slurs his words, and makes moronic comments, and tries to tell some lame jokes. Half the time, nobody can understand what he's talking about, so we just try and talk around him. Then he gets angry because he's not getting all the attention he craves. But, of course, he's not an alcoholic; according to him, he's just a guy who likes to have a good time—and make everybody else miserable."

Greg felt very close to his wife, Anita, but Vic's antics repeatedly impinged on what should have been a joyous time for them. Anita had a typical alcoholic family, which had never acknowledged, let alone confronted, that enormous elephant in the living room—the family secret or problem that everyone is aware of but no one is willing to deal with. That problem may be drug abuse, compulsive gambling, sexual aberrations, or any of the myriad other shame-filled behaviors that affect our lives. But whatever form the elephant takes, everyone tiptoes carefully around it, pretending it isn't there.

As the new member of the family, Greg found that he couldn't comfortably play along, but, understandably, he was reluctant to be the one to blow the whistle. I asked him if there was any chance of putting together an intervention in which the family would confront Vic about how his behavior was affecting each of them and what they wanted him to do about it.

"I don't think there's a chance. Nobody wants to talk about it, let alone confront Vic. I pleaded with Anita to go to Al-Anon, but she doesn't like to 'upset people' or say anything negative about anybody in her family. My mother-in-law is humiliated by his behavior, but she's been putting up with it for thirty-two years. She's financially dependent on him, and I think she's also very emotionally dependent. My brother-in-law lives in another state, so he's no help. So where does that leave me? I mean, he's not an abusive drunk, but he's a total asshole, and he ruins every holiday, every family get-together—what should be pleasant occasions. Do

I have any rights here, or do I just have to keep pretending that everything's fine, too?"

Greg was the only one dealing even remotely with reality, but that put him in a very precarious position. When a family mobilizes to protect and minimize the addiction of one of its members, it will always see the truth-teller as a villain. I asked Greg if he thought Anita would turn against him and ally even more strongly with her father if he decided to take some action in confronting the situation. He answered that he didn't know, and he didn't know if he was ready to risk finding out. Then a dramatic turn of events forced the issue.

At our session the following week, I knew something had changed. I saw a different man—determined and committed to no longer accepting this unhealthy family system.

"Something happened the other night that scared the hell out of both of us. We have a one-year-old, Michael. We were over at my in-laws' for dinner, and Vic was drinking nonstop, as usual. He was really unsteady on his feet. After dinner, we went into the den and Vic started playing with Michael. In all fairness, he's a really nice grandfather when he's sober—those times are getting fewer and fewer—but that night he was playing too rough with Michael, and knocked him against the coffee table, and the baby split his lip. I was livid, and Anita got as pale as a ghost. As soon as we got the baby's lip to stop bleeding, we left. We barely said a word to each other on the way home, but once Michael got to sleep, I told Anita this is going to stop—now! I'm not going to be a part of this insanity anymore. She nodded her head, and there was a lot of sadness on her sweet face, but she took my hand and told me she agreed. We just don't know how to go about it so we don't hurt anybody and maybe even do irreparable damage to the family."

WISHING, HOPING—AND STUCK

There was a new alliance between Anita and Greg that bodes well for their relationship. Unfortunately, it took a near disaster to get Anita to break through her own denial of how toxic and dangerous the situation with her father was, and to admit that Vic had already done years' worth of damage to his family.

When Anita joined Greg at his next session, it quickly became clear that, for years, she had played the role of Dad's confessor and protector, even though many times she couldn't invite friends over because of her father's embarrassing behavior. Like Dana, Anita fed herself a steady diet of wishful thinking.

"I could never give up the hope that one day he would recognize he had this problem, enter a treatment program or AA, and become sober. Then he would be the dad I knew before alcohol started destroying his brain—the one who was my pal."

Wishing and hoping for her dad to magically change kept Anita passive and ensnared in her father's self-destruction. For years, she had been unwilling to do anything about her own problems with her father, but at least she knew she had to protect her son.

In both Dana's and Anita's relationships with their difficult parents, there was a significant amount of role-reversal. The child became the fixer, the protector, and the rescuer—all part of a parent's job description. Meanwhile, the parents got to abdicate adult responsibilities and manipulate the child into being a savior for them.

There was a strong possibility that Vic might never change. But Anita and Greg would learn how to avoid being victimized by his alcoholism. Together, we would find the words to say and the necessary behavioral strategies that would allow them to set uncrossable boundaries with Vic. Of course, Vic wouldn't like it—but he'd had things his own way for much too long. It wasn't going to be easy, but both Greg and Anita realized there was really no acceptable alternative.

THE NEVER-ENDING BAILOUT

Alcoholism is only one form of compulsive behavior that can create enormous pressure in your marriage. Some in-laws create terrible conflict between you and your partner by expecting you to constantly rescue them from financially reckless and irresponsible behavior.

A balding and gentle-looking forty-year-old stockbroker named Steve came to see me because he knew he was being pulled deeper and deeper into the quicksand by his financially irresponsible in-laws.

"Ever since I got into this family, all Andrea and I have done is bail out her parents from one stupid get-rich-quick scheme after another. I don't know what it is with these people. They have no savings because her father has been day-trading—against my advice—and he's way up one day and way down the next. He's got all kinds of elaborate and risky deals he's involved with, but, if you ask me, it's nothing more than pure and simple gambling. He thinks he's too smart to work, the way the rest of us do. The few times he has hit something, he immediately put the money in the next scheme. Andrea's mom, Lois, has a job in an insurance office, and Stan goes through her salary, too. He knows better than to come directly to me for money, so the game is that every few months he has Lois call Andrea in panic—the mortgage check bounced, or the car's going to be repossessed, or some other catastrophe is about to befall them. And Andrea just gets supercalm, and she gets real parental, and says, 'Well, we'll just have to help them—we can't let them suffer.' No matter what I say, she writes the check. No discussion, no nothing."

Steve and Andrea had wound up in the role of parents, and Andrea's highly dysfunctional parents had become their children. Just as in the other families we've met in this chapter, they wound up rescuing, enabling, and in the inevitable role-reversal—all of which are only a Band-Aid that can't begin to repair the in-laws' very toxic behaviors.

THE DIFFERENCE BETWEEN HELPING AND RESCUING

If you're like Andrea and Steve, what your partner calls "help," you see as rescue, so let's clear up some definitions. Of course, there's nothing wrong with helping a parent or in-law out if they hit a rough spot in their lives. Illness, divorce, loss of employment, and financial setbacks are all part of life. There are times when an offer of money or emotional support may go a long way toward helping someone you care about get back on their feet.

But it's one thing to help an in-law who has a track record of responsible and conscientious behavior. It's quite another to regularly have to bail out an in-law who is always getting into financial trouble through impulsive or ill-conceived overspending, gambling, or reckless investments. Financially reckless in-laws not only expect you and your partner to come to the rescue, they leave you little choice. Your partner's misplaced compassion, combined with the pressure of your in-laws' pleas and dire predictions of what will happen to them if you don't help, make it difficult, if not impossible, to refuse them. But it was getting a lot less difficult as far as Steve was concerned:

"We're draining our savings. This can't go on, and I'm not going to let this guy spend our money the way he spends his. Andrea told me last night that they don't have the $2,500 to make their mortgage payment. Well, tough beans! Let the goddamn house go into foreclosure if they can't afford to keep it. I just don't know what to say to Andrea anymore. I'm so tired of hearing 'They're my parents—we have to bail them out.' "

I knew that Steve was as angry at himself as he was at his in-laws for letting this situation continue to erode his and Andrea's life. His in-laws weren't mean or critical like many we've met, but their inability to manage their own lives was every bit as destructive to his marriage—if not more so. I also knew his brave words would probably not be followed up with brave action. I decided to try a quick fix with him in the hope that it might give him something to hold on to until we could make some major inroads into this mess.

JUST SAY "NO"

I asked Steve if he could say "antidisestablishmentarianism," and he looked at me as if I had just flipped out.

"Indulge me," I said. "You'll see where I'm going with this."

He repeated the word, but he looked extremely skeptical.

"Steve," I remarked, "you've just said the longest word in the English language without any trouble. Why are you having so much difficulty saying one of the shortest?"

He was quiet for a moment and looked puzzled. Then he said, "Oh—I get it—you mean, 'no.' But it's not that easy. There's no emotion with the long word, and there's a lot of emotional heat around saying 'no' under these circumstances, not to mention guilt and the fact that everyone will be mad at me, especially Andrea."

I told Steve I was going to ask him some tough questions that I wanted him to answer.

SUSAN: "Is your helping really changing anything?"
STEVE: "No."
SUSAN: "Do Andrea's parents take any responsibility for getting some debt counseling or attending a Twelve-Step program like Debtors Anonymous or Gamblers Anonymous?"
STEVE: "No way."
SUSAN: "Have you ever seen one penny of what you've given them?"
STEVE: "Are you kidding?"
SUSAN: "I take it, that's a 'no.' OK—so is throwing money down this bottomless pit accomplishing anything, other than encouraging your father-in-law to behave like a lunatic and everyone else to behave like a victim?"
STEVE: "Nope."
SUSAN: "If you gave them a million dollars tomorrow, how long do you think it would take before things were right back to square one?"
STEVE: "Probably about three months—four at the most."
SUSAN: "Last question. Are you the Bank of America?"
STEVE: "Stan thinks I am. . . ."

At this point, Steve put his head in his hands and let out a deep sigh. Then he picked his head up and said:

"I can't let Andrea's parents ruin our future. We've even put off having children. . . . God, I feel like such an idiot! OK, coach—I'm ready to do something about this."

Steve realized that it made no sense at all to be shoring up the lives of troubled, self-absorbed adults who are perfectly capable of taking care of themselves—or might learn to be if his partner would just let go of the anchor that was pulling both of them down. I suggested to Steve that the first thing he needed to do was to sit down with Andrea as soon as possible so they could start bringing sanity and reason back to their lives.

THE SEXUAL PREDATOR

In-laws of both genders are often flirtatious and seductive with their child's partner, other relatives, and, sometimes, with their own children as well. This behavior is often described in ridiculously benign terms like "Oh, Mom's just strutting her stuff," or "Dad's always been a real stud," or "Mom's always gone for young guys," or "You know how men are." These rationalizations and many more like them are designed to discount and diminish the seriousness of such behavior and put a humorous spin on it. But despite the concerted efforts to make light of sexually offensive behavior, it's not funny. It's not cute, it's not charming, it's not playful, and it certainly is not OK. But if everybody just looks the other way and pretends nothing is going on, then the status quo can remain unchallenged and nobody is upset—except, of course, the target.

Kim, a twenty-five-year-old video store manager, came to see me because, she said, she was afraid to be alone around her father-in-law anymore.

"My father-in-law, Phil, has always been a little too affectionate with me, and I'm very uncomfortable around him. A lot of times when we're leaving their house after an evening with them, he hugs me too tightly and stands way too close. I swear, he had an erection the other night. I've been real hesitant to say anything about it, but now it's gotten totally out of control. The other night, we had them over for dinner and he jumped up to take the dishes into the kitchen because I was there. He put the dishes down on the sink and grabbed me and kissed me. He stuck his tongue practically down my throat. He was breathing really hard and he said he's wanted to do that and a lot more since the first time he saw me. It was sickening! He's a good-looking guy and he's only about fifty, but, my god, he's my father-in-law! It's like incest!"

I told Kim I knew she must have felt dazed by what happened. I asked her if she was able to say or do anything.

"I was so stunned and revolted, I went almost catatonic. I started putting the dishes in the dishwasher like a robot. And Phil casually went back to join the others."

Phil was one hundred percent responsible for his behavior, and Kim was one hundred percent not responsible for what happened. But without realizing it, when Kim failed to take action the first time Phil started hugging her in ways that made her uncomfortable, she gave Phil tacit permission to test the waters and see just how far he could go. I told Kim that when we accept the unacceptable without protest, we are teaching the other person that our boundaries are very weak. They then believe that there's nothing to stop them from escalating their offensive behavior.

But there was no reason for Kim to have to fight this battle alone, or so I thought until I urged her to tell her husband, Eric. Kim's eyes flashed with anger when she answered me:

"Oh, I already have, and he said he had no idea what to do. Then Eric told his mother, who says *she* doesn't know what to do. So where does that leave me? Turns out, his father has a history of being seductive and inappropriate with female relatives, so this kind of stuff has happened before. The worst of it is that nobody wants to confront Phil. Eric is more concerned that he will embarrass his sicko father, and that he and his father will be alienated, than he is about me. I just can't believe his damn father's feelings are more important to him than mine. I feel violated and betrayed, and nobody will stand up for me. I love my husband, or did, until he turned into a marshmallow, but I don't think I want any part of a family like this."

Once again, what could have been a good relationship was teetering on the edge of the cliff because an in-law was being allowed to behave badly, and the target of that behavior was hurt and angry because her partner wouldn't take the necessary steps to become her ally. Eric had turned instead into a jellyfish, immobilized by his fear of upsetting his father and being accused of creating a family crisis.

MAKING A FAMILY SAFE AGAIN

If such behavior isn't dealt with as soon as it occurs, in an "I mean business" manner, it will almost certainly escalate, as Kim found, to an invasion of your physical boundaries. Families like Eric's are not safe places until you, with or without your partner, take active steps to stop this kind of behavior. You should not have to fend off unwanted sexual advances, whether verbal or physical, from an in-law any more than from anyone else.

Phil had long operated from a belief that everyone would continue to look the other way. He had a big surprise in store for him once Kim and Eric started coming into counseling together.

WHEN YOUR IN-LAWS HAVE ABUSED YOUR PARTNER

As we move toward the darkest of in-law problems, we run into the turbulent currents that churn beneath the surface of families who have severely mistreated their children. Several of you are married to someone who has been emotionally, physically, or sexually abused as a child. Unlike the needy or inadequate parents in this chapter, some abusive parents do just fine in the outside world. While some may turn to you for help in the arenas we've already visited, others may not need any help or rescuing from you at all. But their past behavior is a sure sign of deep emotional disturbance just below the "normal" façade. So while they may not constantly be in some kind of trouble, your partner's inability to psychologically separate from them will wreak every bit as much havoc in your life. And with these parents, your partner, not you, is the target of their attacks.

WHEN YOU BECOME THE BUFFER

Mel, a short, thirty-one-year-old dispatcher for a trucking company, sought me out because, as he put it, "I'm tired of being in the middle between my wife and my in-laws." At our first meeting, he explained:

"Jenna has me screen calls from her parents. They are really critical and insulting to her, and always have been. Her father used to beat her when she was little, and lock her in the closet for hours. She was six years old, for chrissake! How could anybody do that to a little girl? Then her wonderful mother blamed her for whatever tension and anger there was between the two parents, and, I'm sure, there was plenty—there still is. I knew they were going to be a problem when we started dating, but Jenna's seemed so strong—a real survivor. I just thought she could take care of herself."

Mel had incorrectly assumed that because all this happened in the past, Jenna had outgrown the traumas. But once they began their life together and had to deal with her parents regularly, he discovered that her strength was really a façade she had erected over the years in order to function in the world. Inside, she was still a frightened little girl.

If your partner has taken the essential steps toward healing and individuating (and, unfortunately, Jenna had not), then your relationship with your in-laws will most likely not create major problems in your life. But if those conditions haven't been met, you will inevitably be caught in the middle without a clue as to how to act around people who have deeply hurt someone you love. And to make matters more confusing, your partner will frequently balk at any attempts you make to protect her or him.

"She's always really upset after one or the other calls her up. I don't know why they do—they're terrible to her. Lately, she just doesn't want to talk to them, so I end up having to lie and say she's not here, or I'll have her call you back, which she rarely does, so then I get blamed for trying to keep them away from her. She's so frightened of them, it kills me to see it. I want to tell them to take a long walk off a short pier and leave us alone, but she won't hear of it. She swears she'll stop using me as a buffer as soon as she gets a little stronger. Do you believe she still has these fantasies that someday, somehow, she's going to make things OK with them? I don't want to spend the next twenty years in this crazy routine. I don't understand why she doesn't tell them the truth about how she feels about them, or just tell them to go to hell."

Mel was understandably bewildered by Jenna's need to maintain a relationship with the people who had caused, and continued to cause, so much pain. To him, the solution to the problem was so clear: Jenna tells them to knock off the put-downs and abusive phone calls or she's going to cut them out of her life.

But Mel needed to understand some basic truths about adults who were abused as children so that he could change his bewilderment and impatience to wisdom and compassion.

THE LEGACY OF ABUSE

As we've seen, almost all in-law problems flourish in a climate where your partner has major unresolved conflicts with his or her parents and has been unable to psychologically detach from them. That allows your in-laws to have a much more prominent role in your lives than is healthy. And there is nothing more likely to impair a person's ability to break free of his or her parents and become a confident adult than childhood abuse.

Abuse decimates self-esteem. It cripples confidence and fosters self-doubt and self-hatred. People who've suffered abuse do not believe in themselves or their abilities. They do not feel entitled to good things or real love. They cling to the people who have mistreated them because, at their core, they still feel like bad, unworthy little kids who truly believe they must, as irrational as it may sound, get their parents to love them before they can move on with their lives.

Mel wondered if Jenna could ever heal from her childhood, and I assured him that this was not at all a dead-end street. As traumatic as these experiences are, and despite all the gloomy predictions you've probably heard that people who have been abused become damaged merchandise forever, it simply isn't true. After more than two decades of working with adults who had been abused as children, I could tell him unequivocally that, with hard work, this damage can be dramatically diminished. If Jenna were genuinely motivated to unhook from her parents, she could reclaim much of her self-respect, which would pay huge dividends in her marriage. There was much to be done, but with Jenna's active participation, and his, they would learn how to take thoughtful and effective action with her parents.

THE DYSFUNCTION MAGNET

Throughout this chapter, no matter what form your in-laws' dysfunction takes, you have seen that the worse the parents' addiction, or abuse, or inability to cope with their lives and the world, the less the adult child is able to pull away. After many years of rescue fantasies, and after supporting, caring for, encouraging, and cleaning up after inadequate, irresponsible parents, your partner believes that it is his or her duty to do whatever it takes to rescue a parent in difficulty. Then, the fantasy goes, someday the reward will come: Your in-laws will finally deliver the love and approval that your partner craves so desperately.

Your partner's urgent need to rescue your in-laws is not a conscious choice. It is a deeply ingrained response to years of living in crisis and surviving by taking care of the parents' needs instead of the other way around.

PRESSURE DOESN'T WORK

It's easy to feel resentment toward a partner who has dragged you into the morass of life with chaotic in-laws. You know that if you and your partner encountered strangers like this on the street or in a social situation, you'd almost reflexively back away and put as much distance as you could between you and them. With clear, objective eyes, you see your in-laws as having taken advantage of your partner, and you see no end in sight.

But tempting as it is to reach for a quick solution and pressure your partner into cutting off contact with your destructive in-laws, it won't really solve anything. It will only reinforce your partner's sense of him- or herself as an inadequate child without choices or options. As you'll see in the second half of this book, it's far more effective to support and encourage your partner in coming to terms with his or her parents in the here and now. Then, and only then, will he or she have a real chance to make new choices and to make you and your marriage top priority.

6 The Rejectors

The darkest of the toxic in-laws we'll meet are those who have totally closed their minds and hearts to you and would, if possible, close you out of their lives. These are the rejectors—the in-laws who regard you as unacceptable. You are not what they wanted (and they couldn't care less that you're what your partner wanted), and they rarely miss a chance to let you and your partner know it, often in cruel and incredibly unfeeling ways.

Rejectors take every opportunity to push you away, baiting you to get out of the marriage they've made so intolerable. To underline how much they'd like to sever any connection with you, they're highly likely to issue invitations to your partner while excluding you and, in some cases, even their own grandchildren. In the most extreme cases, they withdraw their love completely from their child as well, exiling you both from the family. Better to have no child at all than one who will not give them the compliance they have to have.

The reasons they give for rejecting you are many and varied, and often have little to do with the real forces below the surface that are causing them to act in such hurtful ways. They claim they don't like you because they can't tolerate your family, your social or economic status, your religion, your race, or, in my client Holly's case, even the way you look.

EARLY WARNINGS

Holly is a thirty-four-year-old loan processor with a large mortgage firm. She has a pretty face framed by soft, curly auburn hair. And, by any standard, she is quite overweight. She and her husband, Preston, an insurance claims adjuster, came to see me after two years of marriage, not sure they would make it to three. A big part of their unhappiness had to do with Preston's parents' horrible behavior toward Holly, which started long before they got married.

"Preston's the only man I've ever been with. We were high-school sweethearts, and things started getting serious when we were in college. He started staying overnight at my apartment, and that's when his parents turned on me. They were OK to me until they saw that I was a threat to their close-knit family unit. His mother would call him at my place, and when I answered the phone, she would hardly say anything to me, except, 'Put Preston on the phone.' It was as if I didn't exist. To make things worse, Preston quit college to go to work full-time and didn't tell his parents. When they found out, they were furious and said I was the reason he didn't finish school. I had plenty of warnings that things were going to be difficult, but I figured I could handle it. I felt sure that once they got used to the idea that we were serious, and they got to know me, things would get better. Boy, was I in a dream world!"

TIME DOESN'T HELP

Remember the myth of "once they get to know me, they'll like me"? We all want to believe that our love for our partner will touch even the stoniest in-law, and Holly, like so many others who have felt the sting of their prospective in-laws' rejection, was certain that Preston's parents would come around once they saw how much she and Preston cared for each other, and realized that she was a good, loving person. But most rejectors aren't easily moved from their gut-level opposition to you. In fact, the more Preston's parents saw how much love the couple had, and how little they could do to change their son's mind, the more they intensified their warfare against her.

"When Preston told them we were getting married, they said they wouldn't come to the wedding. He told them he was going to marry me regardless of what they did, and they finally ended up coming. But my mother-in-law did something I'll never get over—she stayed seated while we were saying our vows, even though everyone else was standing—as her way of protesting the marriage! Through all of this, my father-in-law just remained quietly in the background and went along with everything she did."

THEY ATTACK WHERE YOU'RE WEAKEST

Some in-laws may be disappointed with their son or daughter's choice and make some effort to change their child's mind. Then, once the marriage actually takes place, they may soften somewhat, accept the inevitable, and even make some effort to be nicer. They may not be happy, but they maintain the emotional bond between themselves and the new family, even if that bond is marred by criticism or efforts to control the relationship. Preston's parents, however, were dyed-in-the-wool rejectors—no softening or acceptance here. After the wedding, they took another tack—they zeroed in, with laser-like accuracy, on Holly's greatest vulnerability:

"The major area for criticism is my weight. I'm definitely heavy, and I'm trying to do something about it, but I certainly don't need Judy's constant comments like, 'You should lose weight,' and 'Why did you let yourself get so heavy?' She never misses an opportunity to mention that someone is getting married to a 'beautiful, slender girl.' Every time she saw me, she would look me up and down as if I were under a microscope. I never knew what to wear—I'd change my clothes five times when we were going to see them. Why does she need to knock me down all the time?"

Holly bore the brunt of the cruelest rejection, but Preston didn't get off scot-free. If you needed any more convincing that toxic in-laws were and are toxic parents, you need look no further than what Preston told me next:

"She knocks me down, too. Holly and I both work really hard, but we never seem to be able to save anything—unlike my father, who's made a lot of money as a businessman. When I said I was thinking about going back to school to finish up my degree, she said, 'You're too old to go back—you've missed your chance.' "

CRISIS TIME

Judy's behavior put an almost unbearable strain on Holly and Preston's marriage, which manifested itself in constant arguing and an atmosphere crackling with tension and resentments. Though he couldn't miss seeing how his mother actively mistreated his wife, Preston did little to give Holly the kind of safety net she needed, and Holly didn't know how to ask him for it. It probably took all of Preston's inner resources to handle his parents' criticism of him while he tried to keep some kind of tenuous peace in the family.

Then, about a year into the marriage, for whatever reason, he chose to deal with his internal struggles in a way that not only mirrored the rejection Holly received from Preston's family but was far more devastating to her.

"Preston had an affair with a woman at work. It didn't last very long, but when he finally told me about it, I was devastated. And, of course, it magnified my insecurities about my appearance a thousand times. We're putting our lives back together, and coming to see you is a big part of that. He knows I'm still angry, and I'm terribly hurt, but he's starting to open his eyes and really see what's going on. I know he wants this marriage to work."

I asked Preston if that was true. He said "yes" without hesitation.

I asked them to each make a list during the next week of the three most important things each of them could do to help reach that goal.

At our next session, Holly told me that they had agreed it would be important to move to another part of the city, which would be closer to work for both of them and a lot farther from Preston's parents.

The next item on Holly's list related to important changes she needed to make in her own behavior. As Holly told me:

"I've always been very shy and meek. But I know I have to change to survive. Judy just sent an Easter card addressed 'to my son only.' I worked up all my courage and decided to have it out with her. I called her up, but she hung up on me. Now she's finally realized I won't take this crap, and she complains to Preston that I'm too strong!"

To which Preston responded, "Well, let her complain—it's her biggest joy in life."

For his part, Preston was presenting solid evidence that he was willing to work hard to strengthen his marriage. He:

1. Agreed to come to counseling regularly
2. Recommitted to a monogamous relationship
3. Accepted full responsibility for the affair and the effect it had on his wife

And, not least of all,

4. He stopped defending his parents' behavior

He also changed his old pattern of internalizing all the conflicts and then exploding, and took the positive action of agreeing to move to a different neighborhood.

The pain left in the wake of Preston's affair would take a while to diminish. But I believe that the affair was a powerful wake-up call for him to examine his behavior in all aspects of his relationship to Holly, especially in regard to his parents, because he came very close to losing her.

Preston and Holly are working hard in therapy and they

are doing well. Holly is attending regular meetings of a national weight-loss organization and has dropped thirty pounds already. At a recent session, Holly said something very poignant that showed how deep the wounds of an in-laws' rejection can be:

"You know, things are so much better with Preston and me, but there are times when I still feel really cheated. My two sisters have wonderful in-laws, and sometimes I slip back into thinking, 'Why am I not good enough—all I did was love their son.' "

"Wrong question, Holly," I answered. "The real question is, why aren't they good enough to see what a terrific person you are?"

THE ISSUE OF RACE

Appearance played a big role in Felicia's parents' rejection of her partner as well, but for very different reasons. Felicia, a stunning thirty-two-year-old, is an account executive at an advertising agency. She had begun dating, and, ultimately, had fallen in love with Les, one of the vice presidents of the agency, who was as smitten with her as she was with him. Sounds wonderful, doesn't it? There was only one problem, and it turned out to be a major impediment in their plans for the future: Felicia is white and Les is black.

As Les told me:

"The first time Felicia brought me home was almost the last time. Her father took one look at me and said, 'I don't know who you are, but I do know what you want. So let there be no mistake about it—you are not welcome in this house and there's no way on god's green earth that you're going to marry my daughter.' Felicia started to argue with him, but I wasn't willing to play that game. I just took her arm and said, 'Let's go,' and we did."

Some of the most violent rejections come from prospective in-laws who are blind to anything about you but an essential, unalterable part of who you are—your race. Just the sight of you triggers strong, negative reactions that seem to be bone-deep. If this is your situation, you have, no doubt, dealt with this kind of hostility before, but it's doubly painful when it comes from the family of the person you love.

It would have been wonderful if the first time Felicia brought Les home, Chandler had been able to say something like, "I'm not at all happy about your choice, and I can't pretend that I am. I think you're going to have a difficult time. But I also see how much Les loves you, and love is a rare and precious commodity. I guess I'll just have to get used to the idea, so please be patient with me. I wish you both the best."

I told Les I understood how painful it must have been to not hear those words, or others like them, from Felicia's parents, or not to be given the chance to show what kind of man he was and to melt the ice around their hearts.

And, certainly, that was what Felicia had hoped for, because she had never seen this side of her father before.

"My father has black friends! We were brought up to be as respectful to them as we were to the other adults in our lives. But, I guess, it's different when it's a lot closer to home. So I didn't know what to say. I was mortified—and furious. My mom was mortified. I was terrified this could break us up, but Les was wonderful. On the way back to my place, he said he couldn't see how a man who had raised a daughter like me could be all bad. And, I guess, we pretended things would be OK, but it got worse before it got better. My dad just wouldn't stop. He would call me and say the most derogatory things about Les. A couple of times, I just hung up on him, which made me feel absolutely awful. There were a lot of times I wondered if I could really handle this. I just wanted to run away from all the tension and bickering. But the more he tried to push me away from Les, the more determined I was to hang in there."

I urged Felicia and Les to do just that, regardless of how her parents, especially her father, behaved. I had seen several mixed-race couples destroyed by the bitterness and hurt that this particular form of rejection can cause.

Mixed-race relationships and marriages are, by their very nature, complex. They force people to confront their deepest, often suppressed feelings about differences and stereotypes—feelings you can often see in the faces of friends and other relatives besides your in-laws. There's no denying that there is a lot more acceptance in our culture for marriages between people of different races and religions than there used to be, but, like it or not, the reality is that these differences are still a hot button for many people—especially when it involves their children's choice of a partner. And it's a button that Les had pressed with his prospective in-laws.

REJECTION FROM THE GRAVE

Earlier in this book, I mentioned that the different in-law categories are not sharply delineated, and many in-laws exhibit behavior that crosses more than one category. In chapter 4, you saw how Norm tried to exert control over many aspects of his daughter Shelley's life. In a macabre twist of fate, Norm became among the cruelest of rejectors as well—and money was his weapon of choice.

About two months after David and Shelley started seeing me, Norm died of a heart attack during a tennis game at his club. In the aftermath of his death, it was finally impossible for Shelley to maintain any illusions about her father and the depths to which he was willing to go both to reject David and to punish Shelley for marrying him. As Shelley told me through her tears:

"He never loved me! You don't do this to someone you love! He left everything to my mother and two brothers and had a clause in his will that stated unequivocally that I was to be given nothing. And there wasn't even a token bequest for his only grandchild. I don't care about the money—it would have been lovely to have had some of it, but we'll be fine."

I told Shelley that Norm had reached out from the grave to accomplish two things: He punished Shelley for leaving him by using his money as a club, and he made sure that there was nothing of his she could share with his detested rival.

Shelley listened quietly and, after a moment, she turned to David:

"Sweetheart, I am so sorry that I put you through so much because I couldn't bear to face how awful my father really was."

Norm had never accepted David—and it's highly unlikely that he would have accepted anyone his daughter chose. His smoldering resentment of the man who had taken his prized possession from him manifested itself not only in control, but in callous rejection, as well.

THE HIDDEN AGENDA

There was a powerful subtext to Norm's stated reasons for rejecting David, which became clear after David told me some vitally important history:

"Shelley confided in me after we got married that when

Norm found out about me, he came over to her apartment and harangued her until four in the morning about what a horrible mistake she'd be making. First, it was because I was Jewish, then it was the fact that I was never going to amount to anything. He'd say: 'Get rid of this guy. You can do so much better. You've got a great job, and you know you can always count on me for anything you want. He doesn't have the drive. . . . You'll be stuck in a tract house with screaming kids.' Then he took out his wallet and gave her five hundred-dollar bills to show her who could really take care of her in style. Shelley was ashamed and afraid to tell me about this for fear I wouldn't go through with the marriage. I told her it's a miracle that she did. When I first met Norm, I thought he was just a typical overprotective father. But now I realize how sick this man is. He really wanted to be the only man in Shelley's life."

David hit it right on the nose. Norm seized any opportunity to show his daughter that her husband was not the man her father was—not as rich, not as ambitious, definitely inferior. Norm was so fused with Shelley that there were no boundaries or clear role-definition. His jealousy of any man who threatened to diminish his role in Shelley's life made him compete with and belittle anyone who tried to take his place. But what was his role and what was his place? Was he her father, or was he a rival for her affection with any man who came along?

In all this blurring of roles, there is a strong theme of seductiveness and confusion. It was very painful for Shelley to admit to David and to me that her father had always been flirtatious and inappropriate with her. Most of all, it was painful for her to admit it to herself.

"NOBODY WAS GOOD ENOUGH FOR ME EXCEPT HIM"

"I'm starting to realize that he had no concern for what I wanted or what I felt—he only cared about himself. I could have brought home Mel Gibson and it wouldn't have made any difference. It wasn't that no one was good enough for me—it was that the only man who was good enough for me was him. Thank god, he never actually did anything sexual to me, like what happened to some of my girlfriends, but he was always kidding around about sex, and when I started dating, he wanted all the details of what I was doing with my boyfriends. You know, I really adored him, but I always felt uneasy with him."

While Norm may not have acted out his unhealthy feelings for his daughter in overt physical ways, the climate that he created between them was certainly one of psychological incest. And while his behavior was not prosecutable, it bound Shelley to him in powerful ways that were just now becoming clear to her. In that climate, it was inevitable that he would reject any man who threatened to push him out of the picture.

INCOMPREHENSIBLE CRUELTY

Norm knew how cruel he was being to cut Shelley out of his will. But, in his mind, he was totally justified, because his adored daughter not only defied him by marrying David—she had betrayed him, as well. To him, punishment and rejection were the only appropriate response under the circumstances. In Norm's distorted way of looking at the world, his daughter and son-in-law were the villains and he was the victim. But he would show them—and he did.

There is a fascinating paradox and a great deal of irony to

all of this. Norm thought he could create more pain and trouble with his actions. But he would probably be none too pleased with Shelley's reaction to his final rejection of David, because, in the end, it was Norm who was rejected as Shelley and David went on with their lives. I don't think Norm will ever find much peace, but I know that Shelley and David did.

THE BABY FACTOR

Sometimes, in-laws who have thoroughly rejected their child's choice of partner can surprise you—especially with the birth of a grandchild.

When Felicia and Les had their first child, a marvelous little boy, Chandler didn't want to go to the hospital. But, to their surprise, they got some strong support from an unexpected source: Naomi, Felicia's mother, finally put her foot down.

Les:

"I couldn't believe my mother-in-law. She called me before she came to the hospital, and she was almost giddy. She said that she was waiting for Chandler to change his clothes. Then she told me, word for word, what she'd said to him. She actually stood up to my father-in-law and told him that he was behaving like an idiot. She said to him, 'You have a grandson, and you're the biggest baby in the family. It's time to stop all these things you've been saying and doing and grow up! This man is good to our daughter, and they love each other. I'm pretty ashamed of the way I've gone along with you in this, but no more. I'm going to the hospital in ten minutes. If you're not ready to go with me, I'm going without you and you can just stay home and think about how much unnecessary misery you are creating for everybody for no reason other than that your son-in-law is not what you had dreamed about. Well, I've got news for you—you weren't what my parents dreamed about, either, and I'm sure I wasn't Miss America as far as your parents were concerned!' She said that Chan became very quiet and went upstairs to change his clothes. And, to my shock and astonishment, they both came to see us. Chan was uneasy, but he did hold the baby and said he was a fine boy. At least, it was a beginning."

A WELCOME THAW

Naomi and Chan had reared a child whose heart was open and loving, and it seemed almost impossible that, deep down, they didn't have some capacity for accepting Les, even if it was later rather than sooner. After all, they had something precious in common—they all loved Felicia.

Once Felicia was home, Naomi became very involved with the baby and helped out as much as she could. She began to take great pleasure in being a grandmother and started to form a close bond with her grandson. At first, Chandler was petulant about the time Naomi was spending at their daughter's house, but Naomi told him he was welcome to come over, too—as long as he behaved himself!

Things will never be idyllic between Felicia's new family and her original one, but at least they are calm and civilized. They alternate holidays with Les's parents, and what was once a deep freeze has thawed considerably.

SOMETIMES THE INSULTS DON'T STOP

Felicia and Les's story has a relatively happy ending—not bliss, but peace. It's the outcome that we keep at the back of our minds and don't dare to hope for, but pull out for comfort, nonetheless. And it's extremely painful when, as Noah and Ellen found, even a new baby can't bring a trace of acceptance into your relationship with rejecting in-laws.

Ellen, a twenty-eight-year-old computer programmer, came into her marriage to Noah, a deputy district attorney, with a six-year-old daughter whom she'd had with a former lover.

"It always rankled them that I hadn't been married when Melissa was born. When Noah brought me over and introduced me to his parents, they seemed nice enough, but things got strange when Noah mentioned Melissa. 'Oh, you were married before?' his father asked. I said, like I always do, 'No, her father and I were never married.' It was the truth, but I knew immediately it was a wrong thing to say. His father just said something like, 'We don't approve of that sort of thing.' There were some long, awkward pauses after that, and, basically, they've treated me like a tramp ever since. It was pretty clear after Noah and I married that Melissa and I didn't fit in at family events, and we weren't welcome. Melissa is sweet and affectionate, and it's impossible not to love her, but they act like she'll infect the other grandkids by talking about her dad, who's a guitarist in a rock band. She thinks it's exciting. The family thinks it's all sex and drugs and wild living. I've seen Noah's father pull her away from the other kids and send her to watch videos in a room by herself. He's just cruel."

Noah acknowledged that his parents, Stan and Elise, had always been rigidly intolerant of any lifestyle but their own. To them, Ellen was morally lacking and a danger to the good image of the family. Her presence, and Melissa's very existence, seemed to threaten them and everything they stood for. Never mind that Ellen worked hard at a demanding job and was a devoted mother with an exuberant, well-mannered child. Nothing she could do could alter her in-laws' negative opinion of her. She was a symbol of a kind of life that was alien to them. They feared it, and they didn't want Ellen's bad influence to corrupt their family.

For the first two years of her marriage to Noah, Ellen had raged, grieved, and finally told Noah she couldn't take much more—then she found that she was pregnant. They both thought that surely the knowledge they would have a new grandchild would have to diminish the deep freeze with Stan and Elise.

"I know you've heard it all," she told me, "but tell me if you've heard this one. When Noah told them I was pregnant, the first thing his father said was that he'd better get a paternity test, because how did he know the baby was his? No congratulations, no joy, just a nasty, insulting comment implying I probably had been cheating on him."

I told Ellen that I had indeed heard from other clients that their in-laws had made similar remarks. I assured her that it's natural to believe you're the only one in the world that this can be happening to when you run into rejection of this magnitude. Stan and Elise had done everything they could think of to make Ellen's life miserable, no doubt in the hope that she would get fed up and leave Noah. Then they would be rid of this blight on their upstanding family. And they came perilously close to succeeding. Even the birth of a little grandson did nothing to stop their attempts to undermine their son's marriage.

As Ellen told me:

"They haven't seen my kids or me for over three years. They have no photos of us. There are no gifts for the kids."

And Noah added sadly:

"It's just incomprehensible to me that they could continue treating Ellen this way even after we had Noah. He's Noah III, you know—named after me and his granddad.

How could they turn their backs on a beautiful little baby? Ellen's folks have been really generous, but my parents didn't even give us a dime for medical expenses, or bring her a single present. It's one thing to be upset with me—I can handle that—but I can't handle them hurting my wife and children like this. I'm at the end of my rope. I mean, they are my parents, but I can't let this go on. I just don't have a clue as to what to do about it."

I told Noah and Ellen that figuring out a plan of action was long overdue. They had taken years of abuse and had done little to deal with it effectively. Unless they were willing to make some dramatic changes in how they handled this terrible situation, they were facing years of conflict, rage, and the searing pain of seeing even minimal affection denied to two innocent children.

THE EXILE WEAPON: "YOU'RE NO LONGER A MEMBER OF THIS FAMILY"

Of all the threats and punishments that rejectors call on to show you they mean business, perhaps the most devastating is "If you marry that person, you're no longer a member of this family." It sounds like a desperate bluff, but you'd be surprised at how many parents actually reject their own child as the ultimate expression of disdain for you—the person they can't tolerate.

Threats of being exiled from the family, combined with intimations of grim emotional consequences if your partner incurs their wrath, are the heavy artillery of the rejectors. It takes a lot of fortitude to stand up to ultimatums like this. The prospect of emotional exile activates primal abandonment fears and our similarly primal need for bonding and connection. This threat, whether serious or not, can also stir up enormous ambivalence and guilt for your partner about where his or her loyalty and obligation lie.

Hank, a stocky, sweet-faced twenty-six-year-old who is a third-year medical student, had no intention of getting serious about anyone until he was at least into his residency. But that was before he met Nancy, a vivacious redhead who worked in the dean's office. Hank's parents were extremely upset when they realized the relationship was getting serious.

Nancy:

"Hank's parents are very well-to-do. His father, Warren, is chief of cardiology at a large hospital, and his mother, Fay, is a successful interior designer. They belong to the most exclusive country club in the city, and they're members of the board of the symphony and the opera. It's a very prestigious and substantial family. They have relatives who are civic as well as business leaders. It's all pretty overwhelming for me—my family is, basically, shanty Irish. I was really intimidated when I met them the first time, but I certainly didn't expect the reception to be as frosty as it was. After some very forced small talk, Warren asked me if I realized that my relationship with Hank could seriously endanger his ability to finish his medical studies. I felt totally on the defensive the entire evening and I couldn't wait to get out of there."

Nancy had plenty of evidence from the reception she got from Hank's parents that there were big storm clouds on the horizon, but she chalked it up to her own nervousness. She had no idea how much Fay and Warren were enraged by Hank's choice.

"As we were leaving, Warren took Hank aside and said something to him. I couldn't hear what it was, but I could tell by the expression on Hank's face it must have been pretty terrible. Hank was quiet on the ride back to my apartment, and I finally asked him what in the world his father had said to him. He tried to be light about it but it didn't work. 'Oh, nothing much,' he answered. 'Dad just said in his inimitable snobby way, "That girl has absolutely no class or breeding. I can't believe you would go for someone like her, with all the suitable girls you've been out with." When I told him to save his breath because my mind was made up, he said if I marry you I should just forget about ever being their son again. Don't worry about it—he's just throwing his weight around like he always does when something displeases him.' "

But he wasn't. Hank tried to sound unconcerned, but he had no way of knowing if his father would make good on his threat. He was devastated when his parents totally broke off contact with him after his wedding. Nancy urged him to try and reconcile with them, but his attempts were always met with the same condition—"not until you get rid of 'her.' " His parents stopped calling and no longer acknowledged his birthdays and holidays. When Hank's sister graduated college, he was not invited to attend the ceremonies or the party afterward. They acted as if Hank had ceased to exist.

Rejectors like Warren and Fay believe that if they are cold enough, or cruel enough, you, the untouchable one, will get fed up and go away. Using love as a sledgehammer, they express their "concerns" for your partner's well-being by total rejection of you—promising that all will be well again as soon as you're out of the family portrait.

Hank's parents had put him in a "it's her or us" bind. Even though he chose Nancy, the exile from his family took a terrible toll on his emotional well-being. And no matter how hard he tried to convince himself that he'd done the right thing, he found himself wondering if he'd paid too high a price for his marriage. He loved Nancy, but he also harbored deep resentment against her for what he believed she had cost him. It would take a lot of work on the part of the three of us before this young couple could reclaim the love and happiness they deserved.

THE BLINDNESS OF REJECTORS

Obviously, parents whose adult child of any age makes a truly bad choice in a partner—someone who is a substance abuser, financially reckless and irresponsible, who has a terrible track record with relationships and has left many wives and children behind, or has an unsavory or even criminal past—have every right to protest and to do what they can to get their child to see the unhappy reality of the situation. They would be falling down on their job if they didn't.

But none of the targets of rejectors you met in this chapter have the kind of major character flaws or backgrounds that would raise red flags and justify that type of intervention. The flaws lie with the people who reject them and who are deeply threatened by change. Intolerance, rigid expectations, and demands that their children cede them veto power over their marriage, merge to blind them to you as a person who is, at the very least, deserving of courtesy and respect.

They reject you without ever getting to know who you really are.

7

Why Do Toxic In-Laws Behave This Way?

"Why do they treat me this way?"

"Why do they dislike me?"

"Why can't they see how hard I'm trying?"

"Why don't they see how good I am for you and how much we care about each other?"

"Why do they need to hold on so tightly?"

Why? Why? Why?

You have probably asked yourself and your partner questions like these a hundred times. We are an intellectually curious species, especially when it comes to human behavior, and the more baffling the behavior, the more we want an explanation. Your in-laws are full of ready answers—many having to do with your inadequacies and sometimes those of your partner. But the real forces that drive the conflicts are often hidden deep in their unconscious, and the chances that your in-laws will ever unearth them are slim to none. Even if you asked them directly, you'd probably fail to get an answer that means very much. Don't forget that, as far as they're concerned, there's nothing to explain, because, most of the time, they see what they're doing as transparently logical and justified under the circumstances. In their eyes, there's nothing wrong with the way they're acting.

NO EASY ANSWERS

That leaves us to come up with our own exploration, based on what we see and experience, and what we are able to learn about some of the early forces that shaped the behavior that you now find so troubling. Because most of the time we don't have access to our in-laws' inner workings, we'll only be able to find some of the answers, but I believe you'll find them illuminating.

Human behavior just doesn't lend itself to neat, clean explanations because it's determined by many different sources and events. Your in-laws had parents, too, and those parents had parents, all the way back to the beginning of time—so they're playing out a complex family history. They're also responding to a complex web of family beliefs, rules, and expectations that are the genesis of much of their behavior toward you and your partner. And if all that weren't enough, there is the crucial element of their particular genetic loading and temperament—the way they're wired. Their unique physiological and psychological makeup may cause them to be hypersensitive to any real or imagined offense. They may have biochemical imbalances that cause them to be emotionally volatile, highly anxious, or depressed—conditions for which they have never sought any help. They may have a well of anger and resentment inside them that started filling up long before you came on the scene but gets discharged onto you. The behavior that you find so painful often has far less to do with you than with your mother- or father-in-law's individual emotional makeup and history.

Sometimes the fact of your marriage is enough to activate a negative response. Sometimes it takes a personality clash or a set of life stresses. A number of factors trigger toxic in-laws, and if we do a little digging and look more closely at some of the cases we've seen so far, patterns begin to emerge.

THE POWER OF BELIEFS

Your in-laws' problem behavior gets activated in conflicts with you because of the particular interaction between you and their personality characteristics, life circumstances, and, perhaps most importantly, their deeply entrenched beliefs. Problem in-laws, whatever their makeup or type, share a set of beliefs that, individually or collectively, propel their negativity. Why do toxic in-laws act the way they do? Let's shine a light on the most recurrent of the beliefs—some of which are below their conscious awareness—that underpin much of the behavior you find so upsetting. Not every toxic in-law has all of these beliefs, but one or more of them is likely to play a key role in driving the way they respond to you.

1. They Believe They Have a Monopoly on Truth

Several years ago, I had a phone call from my then mother-in-law, whom I'll call Helen. Now, Helen was, to put it as kindly as possible, very difficult and controlling. She had called me up to complain about an argument she'd had with a friend of hers, and after going on for some time about how awful this friend had been to her because of what Helen described as a very minor conflict, she assured me that she had done absolutely nothing to deserve such hostile treatment. Then she asked, "Well, what do you think I should do?" To which I responded, "I don't know . . . after all, there are two sides to every story." Without pausing for even a second, Helen answered: "But I'm telling you both sides of the story!"

This story always gets people laughing when I tell it at speaking engagements. But if you look past the humor, you'll see a gem of an example of the absolutely unshakable conviction held by many people that there is only one truth, one accurate version of reality, one way to look at any situation: theirs. In psychology, we call this a closed system—a mindset and way of perceiving events that prevents many people from exploring alternative ways of thinking or behaving—because they don't realize there *are* alternatives. Many of the toxic in-laws you have met so far firmly believe they have a monopoly on truth, and because of that, they assume they have every right to try to shape you up to meet their expectations.

It's been my experience that the great majority of toxic in-laws share this rigid way of looking at life. And, of course, they resist any outside interference from reality that might challenge their way of understanding their world.

"Different" Means "Bad"

Liz, the child-care aide whose engulfer mother-in-law, Terry, we met in chapter 3, provides a good example of this rigidity:

"Forget about trying to reason with Terry or trying to get

her to see your point of view when it comes to family. She has one set of rules and they're engraved in stone: Family must be together all the time, Family is the only thing that matters, you must sacrifice everything for the Family, when the Family whistles, you jump. If I don't agree and dare to want to do something on our own, I get labeled such charming things as 'selfish' or 'unloving.' And this is the same woman who welcomed me at first with open arms. I guess she thought I was going to be a clone of everybody else."

As Liz discovered, to her mother-in-law, to be different is to be bad.

Reasonably well-adjusted, caring people can allow for differences in beliefs, needs, perceptions, and attitudes. A healthy family could embrace Liz's view that even though family is important, every couple needs its own friends and activities. But for someone like Terry, there is no room for disagreement. Like my former mother-in-law, she believes that only she knows what is true, and blind obedience is the only measure of a person's goodness and worth. None of this makes Terry a horrible person. But her limited capacity for accepting or even acknowledging that she and Liz can disagree on fundamental issues is creating a lot of friction in what could have been a good relationship for both women.

The Tyranny of the "Shoulds"

Throughout this book you've met a lot of people like Terry. They express their opinions about the things that affect you in a variety of ways, but one thing is certain: When you are involved with them, the words *should* and *ought to* and *must* pop up regularly in the conversation. Inflexible in-laws such as these may back up their assertions with religious utterances or statements like "Everyone knows you should spend as much time as possible with family," or "You must always stay home with your child or he'll grow up unhappy." And they often predict the worst for you if your choices deviate from theirs.

In chapter 1, we saw Anne, the graphic designer, bear the brunt of her mother-in-law Vivian's disdain for Anne's career and how she chose to live her life.

"Even though we're doing fine and the kids are wonderful, she's still making these dire predictions about what's going to happen to my marriage and what's going to happen to the kids because I'm working. I don't think she can stand the fact that she was wrong, so she just says, 'You just wait. Wait until your children are older—then you'll see I know what I'm talking about.' I think she'd be secretly glad if something awful happened so she could feel vindicated!"

Rigid opinions, especially those that have your in-laws convinced that they know everything and you know nothing, are almost always wrong-headed because they are usually completely subjective, they don't allow for change or growth, and they don't ebb and flow with life experience. In the face of evidence that the opinions they are holding onto for dear life don't jibe with reality, toxic in-laws will distort reality to make it conform to their truth. Once you grasp just how inflexible their attitudes are, you can stop hoping for some miraculous change and deal with how things are, rather than how you wish they were.

2. They Believe They Are the Center of the Universe

Many, if not most, toxic in-laws are astoundingly self-absorbed, preoccupied with what they want, what they need, what they feel. The self is the only reference they have, and the world must revolve around them, placing them front and center in every situation.

As defined by these in-laws, love is not about acceptance or tolerance. It's about their own emotional comfort level and image. Loving in-laws look at their children and their children's partners and ask themselves:

- How do they enrich my life?
- What do they give me?
- How does what I say or do affect them?
- How can I make the new person in the family feel welcome and at ease?
- How can I work on myself so that the things that bother me about this person are not expressed in hurtful or insulting ways?

But toxic in-laws look at the relationship differently. They ask themselves:

- How do my children and their partners diminish my life?
- What are they taking away from me?
- Will they make me look bad to others?
- Are they a threat to me?
- How can I get my way?

Holly's mother-in-law, Judy, is a classic example of this kind of blind self-centeredness. Judy had never accepted Holly and never missed an opportunity to clobber Holly about her weight. And, recently, she chose a particularly hurtful way of doing just that.

"Preston's brother just told us he's getting married. I was

thrilled because I love the woman he's been with, and I was envisioning helping her with all the things she'll have to do. Then Judy told them not to have me in their wedding because I'm too heavy and it will spoil the wedding pictures. I wonder if she had any inkling of how that made me feel."

Judy's preoccupation with Holly's weight, and her obliviousness to the impact her behavior had, speaks volumes about how self-centered and narcissistic she was. She completely ignored that Holly was a sweet, honest, hardworking young woman who happened to be devoted to Preston. Holly was a threat to the ideal she had created about the woman her son would marry, and a good character was insignificant to Judy, compared with the embarrassment she felt about Holly's appearance and how much Judy believed it reflected negatively on her.

What Will People Think?

Because self-centered people are so dependent on outside admiration and approval, most of them are consumed with how they look to others. Judy imagined that people would see that she was cursed with an overweight daughter in-law. Would they think this was the best Preston could do? What would they be saying about her behind her back? Would they be laughing at her? Or, worse yet, would they feel sorry for her?

It never occurred to her that most people are far too concerned with their own problems to spend much time worrying about how much her daughter-in-law weighs.

Sometimes toxic in-laws' self-centeredness can come perilously close to paranoia. Because everything is about them, they often accuse you of deliberately upsetting them, setting them up for some kind of disappointment or embarrassment, or going out of your way to cause trouble for them in the most innocent situations.

As Pat, the makeup artist whose in-laws had used her husband, Jeff, as their proxy to vent their negativity, told me:

"The other night, Jeff and I were over an hour late for dinner at their house, and the first thing Jeff's dad said when we finally got there was how we never missed a chance to make them wait. He acted as if we had personally arranged for the accident that slowed traffic to a crawl for over an hour and as if I'd deliberately arranged for my cell phone to be on the blink, just to upset them. Is that crazy, or what? You can imagine what the rest of the evening was like."

Most people, on finding out that someone had been stuck on the freeway for an hour, would be at least a little solicitous and compassionate, despite the fact that dinner was late. But self-centered in-laws take everything personally and seem to have little ability to realize that others can be upset and frustrated—not just them. To these in-laws, nobody's feelings matter except their own. They are missing a vital part of their character structure—empathy.

The Missing Empathy Gene

Self-absorbed people lack what I call "the empathy gene." This very precious entity, which cannot be seen under a microscope, is, perhaps, the most important part of our humanness. It resides somewhere inside us—no one knows exactly where. Perhaps in our mind or our sympathetic nervous system, and, unquestionably, in that mass of feelings and sensitivities we call "the soul." It is the part of our being that allows us to feel, or at least understand, what another person is feeling, and to sense how our treatment of that person affects their well-being.

This mysterious, wonderful part of us has been described as compassion, sympathy, understanding, sensitivity, the ability to "tune in," or be able to put yourself in someone else's shoes. I prefer to call it empathy, because, for me, the word "empathy" describes what may be the most important characteristic any of us can possess to help us be truly loving. Empathy gives you the conscious awareness of what someone else is feeling, because you're able to feel some of it yourself, and the empathy gene strongly inhibits the impulse to hurt another person.

Unfortunately, all the rejectors you met in the previous chapter are missing this capacity almost completely, and many of the toxic in-laws that we've seen so far are missing it at least to some extent.

- How could Holly's in-laws have made such cruel remarks about her weight and tried to push her out of family activities if they had even the minimal capacity for putting themselves in her place?
- How could Joe's mother, Ruth, have embarrassed Anne, her future daughter in-law, in front of the guests at the rehearsal dinner with her caustic remarks about Anne's being too ambitious? Didn't she have any sense how much her remarks hurt, and that she was putting a damper on what should have been a wonderful evening?
- How could Ellen's in-laws be so cold and nasty, not only to her but to her daughter from a previous relationship? And then imply, when she got pregnant with their grandchild, that she'd been sleeping around? Did they know how much they hurt her and just not care? In that case, there's a lot of sadistic punishing going on, as there is with many rejectors.

Or did they just lack the sensitivity to recognize the impact of their behavior? Either way, to them, Ellen was not a person with feelings. She was simply a creature who threatened to destroy their fused, unhealthy family system. And that perception allowed them to believe that anything they said or did was justified, because she was the villain of the drama.

- How could Chandler tell Les that he was not welcome in his house because he was black? How did he think that made Les and his daughter, Felicia, feel? Or did he think at all beyond his own disappointment in his daughter's choice? Like most parents, Chan undoubtedly had some ideas that Felicia would marry someone who looked a certain way, or have a background that would make him look good to other people. He measured Les against a set of external standards and found him not only lacking, but a threat to the way Chan wanted things to be. And then he did what people often do when they feel threatened: he attacked. Obviously, Felicia and Les's feelings were of little concern to him at the time.

Some people are so emotionally constricted and so heavily defended, they simply don't have the capacity to walk a block, let alone a mile, in someone else's Nikes. Recognizing and understanding these limitations with both your heart and your head will go a long way toward helping you resolve the question, "How can they treat me this way?"

One of the answers is: They treat you this way because they are either oblivious or indifferent to how much pain they are causing. They cannot feel what you are feeling, and they have a gaping hole inside, where their empathy should be. As a result, they are free to cause suffering without the constraints of such minor inconveniences as guilt or remorse—feelings that would not allow them to go so far without suffering themselves.

3. They Believe That They Can Exorcise Their Demons by Attacking You

Sometimes, you're an unwelcome mirror that reminds one of your in-laws of a part of themselves or their histories they'd rather forget. You may have the misfortune of looking like a sister or a parent they hated when they were kids. Or you may seem like the embodiment of something in themselves they have desperately tried to overcome and forget. In some cases, your very presence can activate an old fear, shame, or unhappy experience. Then your in-laws battle with you as though they are taking on their own demons. The hidden belief is that in attacking you, they're somehow attacking some of their own unresolved problems.

I knew it would be important for Holly to get some insight into Judy as a woman with her own demons and history, so I asked Preston to share as much about his mother's background with Holly as he could. I had a hunch we might find some clues to why Judy overreacted so much to the weight issue and why she continually lashed out at Holly.

The following week, Preston brought in an old family album with pictures of his mother as a child, and one look gave us a lot of answers. In picture after picture, we saw a sullen, very overweight little girl seated between two unsmiling parents. Unwittingly, Holly had activated painful memories and unresolved shame for her mother-in-law, that Judy had pushed away and tried to bury long ago. As we were looking at the pictures, Preston had an important memory:

"When I brought Holly over to meet them for the first time, my mother took me aside in the kitchen and told me I would be in for a lot of cruel teasing from my friends and even other members of my own family. I told her she must be kidding—everybody loves Holly. But she said, almost mysteriously, 'Trust me—I know what I'm talking about.' When I asked her why she was so sure, she changed the subject."

The intensity of Judy's rejection of Holly was a sure sign that Holly had triggered something painful within Judy, and her statement that she'd experienced the same thing herself confirms it. Overreaction is always a sign that the present has become confused with the past. But until they saw the pictures, it never occurred to either Holly or Preston that Holly might have triggered old memories and feelings for Judy. In her discomfort, Judy had made Holly the scapegoat onto whom she could project many of her own lingering insecurities.

Even though Judy was no longer a helpless child, her feelings of insecurity about her appearance were still buried deep inside her. When Holly came into the picture, it was as if the past were suddenly the present, and it gave Judy the chance to change roles—to become victimizer instead of victim.

Acting Out Old Scripts

In addition to reacting harshly to you because of what you inadvertently activate in them, I'm sure it comes as no surprise to you that toxic in-laws are often repeating with you the patterns they experienced as children. Your in-laws weren't born critical, or controlling, or engulfing, or rejecting. They learned these behaviors through their own experiences with people who treated them in those ways. Now, you would think that someone who was constantly put down, or smothered, or made to feel like an outcast would go in the opposite direction as an adult and try to spare someone else ›m feeling the way they did. But, all too often, the opposite is true, and a toxic in-law's behavior with you becomes very much like that of his or her own problem parent.

I learned from Karen that her father, Ray, who was both critical and competitive with her contractor husband, Cal, had a father who behaved in very much the same way:

"My grandfather is almost eighty now, and I don't like him at all—and you know what? I don't think my father does, either, although he'll never admit it. Grandpa is demanding and perfectionistic, and when my father is around him, it's incredible how much he changes in his presence. My big, boisterous dad gets real quiet and turns into a little kid. I couldn't see it before, but I'm realizing, Dad's been the same way with me, oh, maybe not as severe, but he's definitely held up some pretty impossible standards for me . . . and when he's riding Cal, he sounds so much like his own father. You'd think he'd do everything to be different than Grandpa, because I'm sure Grandpa made his life very unpleasant."

It's an old, and, I believe, very valid concept in psychology and in life, that despite our best efforts, we often end up treating others the way we were treated ourselves. As children, we make certain unconscious choices about the messages and role models we are exposed to. If we are harshly treated, there's not a damn thing we can do about it when we're small. So, many people go through a totally unconscious process called "identifying with the aggressor," because that's where the power and safety seem to be. If Daddy is always telling us that what we do is never good enough, or, worse, that *we're* never good enough, many of us, without realizing it, make a decision to be strong and tough like Daddy when we grow up. Then we'll be good enough and nobody can hurt us again. Many people believe, although this belief is usually outside their conscious awareness, that by becoming like the person who hurt them and taking out their early humiliations on someone else, they can somehow help heal the pain they experienced at an earlier time. They create for themselves an illusion of the power they so desperately wanted as a child. And if you're the one who's in their sights, you know how distressing this target practice can be.

4. They Believe There's Not Enough Love to Go Around

Problem in-laws operate from a deprivation mentality. If their child loves you, your in-laws believe you've stolen that love from them. They don't see love as an infinite commodity that replenishes itself the more it's given. And because they're fighting for what they think is a rare and diminishing treasure, each conflict becomes a loyalty test. Your partner must constantly prove that he still is an integral part of their family by preferring them to you, by making them top priority. If your partner doesn't, he or she is in for a barrage of sullen or angry disapproval and hurt feelings from your in-laws.

John, the lawyer you met in chapter 3, gave me a good example of this after he'd tried suggesting that his parents couldn't stay at his house.

"Let's see—some of the choice ones were: 'How can you let her turn you against us?' 'We don't know who you are anymore,' 'This woman has taken your love from us.' When I tried to tell them I still loved them, they wouldn't hear it. Then came the capper—'If you don't have room in your house for us, you don't have room in your heart, either.' "

What John's parents were saying to him, was: "If you love her, you don't have any love left over for us, and not letting us stay with you proves it."

In order to make any sense of these unreasonable demands and absurd accusations, you need to understand how your in-laws really view your marriage. *To them, it's just another version of playing house.* Even if your partner has been living on his or her own for many years, they still don't take your marriage seriously—they've been with your partner for a lifetime, and you're just a newcomer, no matter how long you've been married. Reduced to its fundamentals, your marriage was an act of mutiny—thus the in-laws' constant demand for loyalty tests. The only way for your partner to pass those tests, and avoid awful feelings of guilt and disloyalty, is to override you. Problem in-laws are constantly setting up situations in which your partner is faced with a lose-lose situation. If he puts his parents' wishes first, you feel hurt and neglected. If she puts you first, she hurts her parents.

Saying, in words or actions, that his or her parents count, and you don't, provides the constant reassurance that your in-laws demand. It is as if your partner defines their very life, no matter how accomplished or intelligent they may be. They live through her or him. They are not about to let you take that away.

They Must Hold On to Your Partner at All Costs

All parents naturally want to keep some connection to their children, and if your in-laws were reasonably stable and fulfilled people, they would still look to their children for affection and occasional companionship. But once their children had started a life of their own, they would be able to back off and allow that new life to take root. Of course, even the most conscious, evolved parents will feel a sense of loss and emptiness when a child leaves home, but they will look to each other as well as work, sports, friends, and other relatives to help fill the void. Toxic in-laws, on the other hand, have few other places to look. They probably don't like each other, find little joy in their own marriage, and I've noticed that they often don't have a lot of friends.

As Leslie told me:

"Sal and Gina's whole life is the business, making money, and Tommy. Yet they are always fighting and cursing at each other, both in English and Italian. It's more than just two hot-blooded people letting off steam. They insult and verbally abuse each other like you wouldn't believe. Lots of times Gina calls up in tears. I never hear them talk about going out with other people or planning a trip like normal people. They're like one giant octopus—all wrapped around each other and nobody gets a chance to breathe."

Locked in this crazy marriage, Sal and Gina had always looked to Tommy for their salvation. Their strong, handsome son was the one they could always count on to provide the things they couldn't provide for themselves: attention, companionship, approval, reassurance that they are still needed, and reassurance that they are still in control. For many years, Tommy did just that, and now that there was someone else in Tommy's life, they didn't intend to loosen their hold on him.

In-laws who are intensely enmeshed with their child actually feel betrayed and abandoned when their adult child enters a serious relationship. Tommy had found someone he really cared about and with whom he wanted to build his own family. But instead of being happy about these changes, they viewed Leslie as the person who'd upset the balance of power they had struggled so hard to maintain. As I told Leslie:

"You're a usurper. You've rocked the boat. You've changed the familiar, predictable balance. In Gina and Sal's mind, you took their life away from them, and don't be surprised at the lengths they may go to in order to get it back."

Momma's Boys and Daddy's Girls

You may have noticed that the most intense holding on seems to be between mothers and sons, and fathers and daughters. You've probably also noticed that the most intense conflicts are between in-laws of the same gender: mother-in-law/daughter-in-law and father-in-law/son-in-law. Although there are, of course, exceptions, it seems pretty obvious that jealousy and competition with a younger person who is the same gender as the in-law is especially threatening to a parent who is faced with what feels like an overwhelming loss.

"Momma's boy" and "Daddy's girl" carry a lot more meaning than the somewhat old-fashioned terms indicate on the surface. I'm sure that the Freudians would put all kinds of sexual connotations on this unwillingness on the part of mothers to let go of their sons and fathers to let go of their daughters, but that kind of speculation will do little to help you in the kinds of crises toxic in-laws create in your life.

These terms do, however, tell you a great deal about your in-laws' perceptions and beliefs about who the most important person is supposed to be in your partner's life. They also describe a type of stunted emotional growth on the part of your partner, which can definitely impair his or her ability to truly commit to you.

Pain, Not Pride

Parenting is the only kind of love in which separation, not more closeness, is the goal. For good parents, the child's confident flight from the nest is a stamp of approval on the job they've done. But for many toxic in-laws, this separation, and your partner's ability to bond with you, creates a whole panoply of negative, frightening feelings—abandonment, jealousy, and loss. Instead of being proud of the job they've done, they feel plunged into the unknown, with a fervent desire to pull their adult child back to them so that they can feel the comfort and safety of the familiar again. Only then, they believe, will there be enough love to go around.

BEYOND BELIEFS

So far we've looked primarily at the psychological underpinnings of much of your in-laws' difficult behavior. But as I mentioned at the beginning of this chapter, there are other factors that may play an important part. Physical and biochemical imbalances can play out in controlling, or engulfing, or chaotic behavior, and it can be liberating to realize that the venom that's been directed toward you may have a very real physiological basis, as well as a psychological one, especially when you've been vehemently told that you are the culprit.

As you've seen, in-laws in the throes of addictions or marital and financial crises are so focused on staying afloat that they can't see beyond the next bailout. Things like gratitude or consideration are in very short supply. They feel as if they're drowning, and you and your partner hold the only life preserver. If you don't toss it to them, they may lie, cajole, or try to intimidate you to get their way.

Many addicted, reckless, or depressed people are suffering from an imbalance in their brain chemistry that creates both severe mood swings and irresponsible behavior. All the talk therapy in the world will barely make a dent until the biochemical imbalances are stabilized. Fortunately, there is more awareness of these imbalances as a root cause of a lot of the seemingly incomprehensible behaviors that have been seriously affecting your life and your partner's. There are also more resources for treatment than ever before. The trick, of course, is to persuade the out-of-control person to make use of them.

THE BIG LIE

By now you should have a better handle on why you pose such a threat to your in-laws and why they must level you in such subtly or overtly unpleasant ways. Up until now, your in-laws have had free rein to tell you and your partner that you are the problem. According to them, you aren't good enough, smart enough, good-looking enough, loving enough, rich enough, nice enough, or from the right kind of family or religion, to deserve their love and respect.

And until now you may even have bought into some of their propaganda and believed that you couldn't find ways to get them to be nicer or more loving to you because there was something fundamentally wrong with you.

But, throughout this chapter, you've seen graphic evidence that most serious in-law problems begin with a belief system, and a specific set of characteristics and conflicts that reside within your in-laws, and have little or nothing at all to do with you. I'm not suggesting that you are a candidate for sainthood or that you haven't said or done some really unpleasant things yourself—we all have. But when the intensity of the attacks on you and your marriage are so out of proportion to anything reasonable, it's time to roll up your sleeves and get to work.

The stakes are very high, but so are your chances of success. You can bet the ranch on it.

PART TWO

Protecting Your Marriage

Introduction to Part Two: My Contract with You

Now it's time to tackle new ways of being with yourself, your partner, and your in-laws. To help you do that, I've divided the second half of this book into three parts. In the first section, you'll do some personal work that will help you prepare emotionally for the changes that you, and you alone, can make. I'll help you make a brave and honest acknowledgment of where you get stuck in this triangle, and to see the factors that may be making things far worse for you than they need to be. I'll show you how to get beyond the blaming, finger-pointing, overreactiveness, rage, and the sense of helplessness that serve no purpose other than to make you feel like a victim. I'll help you get beyond that passive, helpless state, to productive change.

Then I'll teach you some powerful strategies for working with your partner. I'll give you the exact words for letting him or her know what you want, and I'll help you create a climate of safety, acceptance, and problem-solving that will give you a significant chance to help your partner ally firmly with you and deal in a more mature way with his or her parents.

In the third section, I'll give you a full arsenal of new, non-inflammatory responses to use with your in-laws, no matter how much they're chopping away at you. I'll also help you set appropriate boundaries with your in-laws and to express clearly, without hostility, what is no longer acceptable to you. In the more extreme cases, where there is little realistic hope that you can penetrate the thick walls of their defenses, I'll show you how to determine and express the consequences for unacceptable behavior—even if that means a moratorium on contact with them—no matter how responsive or unresponsive your partner may be. Finally, I'll lead you toward a place of realistic acceptance, so that you can enjoy whatever is positive in your relationship with your in-laws, without allowing the negative aspects to continue doing damage to you and your marriage.

I know that some or all of these tasks may seem pretty overwhelming to you right now, especially if your emotions are raw from a recent encounter or a long history of difficulties. But just knowing that you have a road map of new strategies and specific guidelines will help you feel calmer. And I can assure you that we'll take this work a step at a time.

If you are not in therapy or have no plans to be, I am going to give you many of the techniques and strategies that I have used throughout the years with clients who have had significant relationship difficulties. If, while you are doing this work, certain strong feelings get stirred up and you would like to explore them further with a professional, I urge you to follow your instincts and do so.

If you are currently seeing some type of mental-health professional or are in a twelve-step program or support group, I assure you that none of this work is designed to replace what you're doing now, but rather to enhance it.

Don't expect things to change overnight. But know that if you do this work, they *will* change, because nothing can stay static once you begin taking action. You will have a renewed sense of confidence and clarity. The tools I will give you in the following chapters will help you step out of the seemingly intractable patterns of toxic in-law relationships and into the freedom of healthier, more loving relationships that you are entitled to.

8

Shifting Your Focus

Those callous, selfish, rotten people.

My wimpy husband.

My infantile wife.

Until now, you've probably been pretty fixated, maybe even to the point of obsession, on who's doing what to you, as each frustrating encounter with toxic in-laws steals another piece of the fun, spontaneity, optimism, and pleasure from your marriage.

And I know that, as a result of these conflicts, there have been painful losses for you. Perhaps you've felt your self-respect, and your respect for your partner, ebb away. Maybe you've had to give up your dream of a close family. You might even have stopped believing that you and your partner are a team, and that together you can handle whatever life throws at you.

REALITY VS. FANTASY

The endless cycle of painful experiences and hurt feelings won't stop until someone has the courage to interrupt it, and I'm sure it won't come as a surprise when I tell you that that someone has to be you. "Why should *I* have to change?" you're probably wondering. "They're the ones with the lousy behavior." But you're the one who is seeing things the most clearly, and you're the one who is the most willing to acknowledge that there are some real problems here. Everyone else seems quite willing to go along as they always have, ignoring the rather formidable dinosaur that is standing right in the middle of the living room.

I know that it would be just great if your in-laws came over one day and said, "We realize how badly we've been treating you. You're really a wonderful person and we owe you a big apology. What can we do to make up for all the bad things we've said and done to you?" And wouldn't it be great if your partner turned to his or her parents during an encounter and said, "Mom and Dad—cut the crap! You are not allowed to treat the person I love this way anymore!" Then you wouldn't have to do anything except bask in this newfound loving family group.

I know that waiting for everyone else to change is a lot more comfortable and less scary than the prospect of having to take action yourself. Unfortunately, it's also unrealistic and, as you've probably discovered, it's futile.

The waiting is over. It's time to act.

A NEW BEGINNING

If you'd been locked in a dark room for a long stretch of time, you probably wouldn't rush out into the light as soon as the door was flung open. The light would be blinding, and the new freedom somewhat disorienting. You probably wouldn't know what to do first.

Along the same lines, I want you to know that you're headed for a new kind of freedom with your in-laws—but you'll want to take some time to get your bearings. I hope you won't be too disappointed if I don't suggest that to start the change process you should run over to your in-laws' or call them on the phone and tell them off. Quite the opposite. The first thing you need to do is slow down and engage your logic and cognition so that you can get some control over the emotions that frequently feel so overwhelming. You need to adjust to the light.

HAVE AN AFFAIR

The first thing you need to do is have an affair. Do I have your attention? You need to shift your focus away from what your partner can't do for you, isn't doing, and didn't do in the past, and away from what your in-laws are doing, have done, or may do tomorrow, to what *you* can do for *you* right now. Steal time in your schedule and rendezvous with the person who knows you as no one else does—you.

It's essential at this turning point that you find some time each day when you can be alone and uninterrupted. Schedule it. Put it on your calendar. I know that if you have small children, a job, a demanding partner, or all of the above, it won't be easy. But it is essential. Even if you have to go sit in a park for an hour, you need to be where you can concentrate on yourself. Take the opportunity right now to do several minutes of self-calming. Meditate, breathe deeply, and tell yourself you are embarking on an important new phase of your life.

THE OBSERVATION ROOM

Once you've carved out your special time and place, I want you to create a mental image that you can use as we work together. Imagine that you are standing behind one of those mirrors used in police interrogations, through which you can see the people being questioned, but they can't see you. From behind the mirror, you can watch the family play out the various scenarios that cause you so much distress.

But something else is going to take place now, because this time you are going to put the spotlight on yourself and see what you are adding to the mix. Whether you're in year one, five, ten, or thirty of the in-law wars, or you've had a recent encounter that's left you full of stormy emotions, I'm going to ask you now to shift your focus from what's being done to you and how unfair it all is, and become a brave and honest observer of how and where you get bogged down in the in-law triangle.

COMMON TRAPS: MISTAKES EVERYONE MAKES

Almost everyone makes mistakes when they're trying to deal with toxic in-laws, and I can guarantee you that no matter how smart and emotionally evolved you are, it's likely that you, too, have fallen into one of the six most common traps:

1. Getting caught up in the victim mentality
2. Overreacting
3. Underreacting
4. Having unrealistic expectations of yourself
5. Having unrealistic expectations of your partner
6. Having unrealistic expectations of your in-laws

I call these categories "traps" because it's so easy to be lured into them, unaware of how much a particular piece of our own behavior can be adding fuel to the conflagration.

We'll look at the first half of the list in this chapter and tackle the final items in chapter 9. You'll notice that I've chosen to make the chapters in this section of the book a little shorter than some of the others. You're going to have a lot of information to handle, and I don't want to overwhelm you by asking you to do too much in any one chapter. Spend as much time as you need with this material, and take it in in small bites. You'll see the most profound changes in your life if you incorporate new insights and skills slowly and steadily.

Trap #1: The Victim Mentality

Mara, the dancer you met in chapter 4, got a healthy wake-up call from a close friend of hers, who helped her see just how easily she had fallen into the trap of thinking, feeling, and behaving like a typical victim, obsessed with how her controlling father-in-law had ruined her dream of a trip to Europe:

"Every time I come across something in the desk that

reminds me of our trip—the travel agent's number or all the beautiful guidebooks we bought—my blood pressure goes up and I'm furious all over again. I didn't realize how much time and energy I was expending on this—or how much of a whiner I had become—until I was out to lunch with my best friend Joan about a week before I decided to start coming here. I started talking about how furious I was with Rob and his father and began going through my litany of injustices again. After a moment, Joan took my hand and said, 'Listen to me—I'm truly sorry you couldn't go, but I'm really tired of hearing about your father-in-law, OK? Quit pissing and moaning about it. You can plan another trip, and if something happens again, I hope you and Rob have the guts to stand up to him. But the trip isn't the real problem, and you know it. The real problem is why you and Rob stay in this situation."

I told Mara that Joan's seeming lack of sympathy was probably not what she wanted, but that, in my opinion, Joan had been not only very wise, but very loving as well. By not supporting Mara's imaginary helplessness with a lot of "ain't it awful" and "poor baby"s, she was actually helping her friend to take the first steps toward getting unstuck. She was also very perceptive in spotting that the canceled trip, as disappointing as it was, was really only a symbol of a much knottier problem.

"You're right, she's right, my parents are right!" Mara exclaimed. "I am stuck! What it all feels like to me is a swamp. I hate the way Jack jerks Rob around, and I hate how much impact he has on our lives. It's turning me into a person I don't like. I call Rob's father horrible names behind his back and I've said some terrible things to Rob, which I really feel awful about. . . ."

I told Mara that if you're walking down the street and

someone knocks you down and takes your money, you're a true victim—someone who has no choice about what happens to them. But in your dealings with even the most monstrous in-laws, you have many choices and options.

"But what are they?" she asked. "I don't have a clue. If I tell Jack off, Rob will be mad at me, and as much of a wimp as I think he's been, I don't want that to happen, and if I—"

"Stop!" I said to Mara. "You're going around in circles. Of course you don't know what to do or you would have done it, and you wouldn't need to be here. You're caught in an emotional spin-cycle of negative thinking, which leads to obsessing, which leads to feeling victimized. Let's start by digging out some of those victim beliefs and replacing them with some workable, realistic new beliefs that are going to feel a lot different and much more hopeful to you."

Changing Hopelessness

I asked Mara to write down the five most recurrent beliefs she had about her situation. After a few moments of thought, here's what she wrote:

- Things will never change
- There's nothing I can do
- Rob's father always wins
- He's ruining our lives
- Maybe I should just get a divorce

Victim beliefs have a sense of hopelessness and finality about them. They are often expressed with words like "never," "always," "can't," and "nothing." And these beliefs seem completely real and valid when you're in the middle of the maelstrom. No wonder Mara was so down and discouraged.

Mara and I then went back to her paper to look for ways to modify her erroneous ideas. For each item on her list, I told her to listen to the wise voice of the person who's stood behind the one-way mirror, watching herself, and add a few words that would challenge the negativity. I told her, the most important thing to remember was that she could only write about what *she* could do—not about what she would like Rob or her father-in-law, Jack, to do. At first, she had trouble moving out of her passivity and negative mood, but soon she warmed to what we were doing, and I watched with delight as her sense of humor and spirit started to return. When we were done, I had her read the new list aloud to me. Here's how it sounded the second time around:

- Things will never change . . . until I get off my butt, quit whining, and do something about them.
- There's nothing I can do. Oh really? It's not going to be easy, and I know things won't get better overnight, but, for god's sake, I'm a person who won a prestigious dance scholarship and a job with a great dance troupe and helped send my kid sister to college. I can't do anything? Give me a break!
- Rob's father always wins . . . Up to now. That's all I'm going to say about that, because he's got some surprises in store.
- He's ruining our lives . . . only if we let him. He's powerful, but not that powerful.
- Maybe I should just get a divorce. Or maybe I should just cool it and realize that this is a wonderful time to learn some new skills and a lot about myself. At any rate, this certainly is no time to make a decision as important as that. Rob

and I still have a lot going for us. We just need to get back on track.

I knew that Mara was sounding a lot stronger than she really felt at that moment, but it didn't matter. It's very important to set goals even though your emotions may be lagging behind. When you do, a fascinating thing happens—the feelings catch up once you start behaving more courageously. If you wait to feel better before deciding things must change, it will take a lot longer.

Mara had set powerful goals for herself that were both realistic and healthy. It would only be a matter of time before she was feeling the confidence she had put down on paper.

I also asked Mara for a commitment in regard to the drinking she'd been doing in an effort to self-medicate her resentment and frustration. Since she didn't have a history of heavy drinking, I asked her if she thought she could stop on her own. She was convinced that the hope and energy she was now feeling would assuage the need to drink. But since she was the daughter of an alcoholic, she also knew she was vulnerable to addiction. She agreed that if she didn't get her drinking under control very quickly, she would attend AA meetings. I told her, that was something we would monitor very closely together, since it's impossible to have the mental and physical acuity needed to do the kind of work she was facing with a mind befuddled by alcohol. As it turned out, the drinking quickly became a nonissue.

Lies Masquerading as Truth

Victim beliefs are lies that we have convinced ourselves are real. They are a source of many of our feelings of impotent rage and helplessness. And, interestingly, it doesn't take months or even weeks to change them. When held up to the light of reality, they dissolve as quickly as a wicked witch under a bucketful of water. They may try and hold on for a little while, but, ultimately, the clarity and strength of the truth will prove too much for them.

Please do this exercise for yourself. Write out your own victim beliefs and then challenge them. Replace every "I can't" with "I haven't yet . . . " For every "never" or "always," substitute, as Mara did, "until now." Read your new list aloud several times. Share it with someone you trust if that feels right to you.

Your beliefs may be similar to or very different from Mara's. Whatever they are, you have the ability, no matter how flattened you may be feeling, to reach that core spark inside yourself and find the antidote to them. Putting the beliefs down in black and white immediately lessens their power. And defining the actions you plan to take, motivating yourself to get out of the victim belief system, increases yours.

Trap #2: Overreacting

Overreactiveness sends blood pressure through the roof. It may take the form of an explosion, a tantrum, yelling, withdrawing into an angry silence, or any of the myriad forms of behavior in which the intensity of the response is way out of proportion to the significance of what triggered it.

An overreaction is hard to miss—when we see it in someone else. But it can be difficult to spot in the mirror because when one of our hot buttons gets pushed, we're convinced we're responding appropriately to a terrible insult. Sometimes it's only in retrospect that our guilt or embarrassment tells us that something else was going on.

Pam, the young artist who designs store windows, was constantly being criticized by her mother-in-law, Sylvia. Some of Sylvia's comments were relatively harmless, but many of them were direct personal attacks on Pam's appearance and adequacy. All of them were unsolicited. Pam typically would withdraw and sulk rather than deal with Sylvia, and as she continued to suppress her resentment, she became hypersensitive to any comment Sylvia made. Finally, it was an almost benign comment that caused her to explode:

"We were setting the table for Chris's birthday party when Sylvia started to change the placement. 'Dear,' she said, 'the salad forks go to the right of the dinner forks.' She sounded so smug and know-it-all—maybe she was just being helpful—I don't know, but what I heard was, 'You can't do anything right. You'll never be the hostess I am,' and I slammed down the forks and broke into tears. I told her to set the damned table any way she wanted to and I went outside to try and calm down. At the time, I thought I was just finally letting my feelings out, but looking back on it, I feel ashamed and foolish. I know that with Sylvia I'm always waiting for the next shoe to drop, but this time, I have to admit, she didn't really do anything so terrible. What am I doing to myself, Susan?"

As Pam and I explored this incident together, she remembered that she had constantly felt inadequate around her glamorous and highly competent artist mother, who missed few opportunities to remind her impressionable daughter how little she could do right.

"Whenever my mother put me down, she'd always start out with this phoney-sweet 'dear,' and then come at me with some belittling criticism. Of course, all I could do was feel terrible and then go to my room and cry. In fact, to this day, if anyone calls me 'dear,' it sets my teeth on edge . . . and what does Sylvia call me when she's being condescending? The same thing, in almost the same tone!"

"Pam," I said. "Ninety-nine percent of the time when a reaction is so out of proportion to the offense, we're responding to something unfinished from our own history and adding that anger to whatever is going on in the present.

"Let me give you an example of overreaction from my own life. When I was a teenager, my mother was obsessed with how I wore my hair, and she was constantly fussing with it and pulling it off my face. This continued even after I was in college, and asking her to stop did no good at all. She even did it in front of my boyfriend, which humiliated me and made me really angry. And guess what—she's still doing it! But now, all she has to do is put her hand anywhere near my face as if she's going to try to change my hair, and I go ballistic. All the old feelings come welling up. I don't even want her to tell me my hair looks nice—I don't want her to be involved with my hair in any way! The difference is that now we can laugh about it. But do you see how those old feelings can get activated by a gesture or a word that serves as a trigger for overreaction?"

Closing the Credibility Gap

If you lose it every time there's a minor offense, here's what's almost certain to happen:

- You'll be seen as hysterical by the people around you.
- Like the boy who cried wolf, nobody will take you seriously when you have a legitimate complaint.

- You'll reinforce your in-laws' position that you are the problem.
- You'll feel embarrassed and inadequate because your emotions are running the show and nobody's really listening to you.

These don't sound like very desirable outcomes to me, and, I'm sure, they don't to you either.

I told Pam that I wasn't suggesting for a moment that she didn't have a right to take action when Sylvia started really digging at her. But that was work we would get to next. What we were talking about in this early stage was learning to separate the minor irritations, like the salad fork business, which can be brushed aside, from the attacks that are really personal affronts, and know the difference.

"But how can I tell the difference at that moment?" Pam asked.

In a time when emotional expressiveness is encouraged, and holding things in, we're told, can actually be harmful to our physical and emotional well-being, it's sometimes difficult to distinguish between an appropriate venting of feelings and falling into the trap of overreacting.

Even if you can't find the genesis of your overreactiveness, all you really need to know is that you can control the outburst you feel coming by stepping back from the purely emotional and becoming an observer of the situation. It takes a little practice but it's worth the effort.

The next time you find yourself about to come unglued, if it's at all possible, excuse yourself, leave the room, and go to where you can get yourself calmed down. Ask yourself the following questions:

- Is what she/he just said cruel?
- Is what she/he just said denigrating to my dignity?
- Is what she/he just said insulting?
- Is what she/he just said abusive?

A lot of comments fall into the salad fork category—irritating and, perhaps, grating, but clearly minor. If that's the case, and you can't answer "yes" to these questions with a straight face, save your emotional energy for the important confrontations. By then you will have learned specific scripts and strategies for dealing face-to-face with your in-laws.

Trap #3: Underreacting

Underreacting is the other face of the factors that lead to overreaction. The anger and the hurt are just as deep, the situation just as fraught with tension, but instead of lashing out, you put a tight lid on your feelings and internalize the negativity that's going on around you. You may deny or rationalize truly grievous episodes or even try to convince yourself that it really wasn't so bad. Anything to avoid an unpleasant encounter and having to do something different than what you're used to doing.

Diane, the department store buyer you first met in chapter 3, had in-laws who insisted on staying at her home for weeks at a time. Her husband John kept giving in to the guilt and obligation that his parents made him feel if he suggested an alternative arrangement, and Diane kept giving in to John. For Diane, the result was an unbending series of migraines and frustrations.

"Susan, I know I'm handling this all wrong. I don't take a

firm stand and I just give in to John's begging. When his parents are there I'm so tense, but I could win an Academy Award for the show I put on. I'm so sweet I make myself nauseous. By the time they leave I'm so stressed out I just want to go to bed for a week."

Diane was describing behavior typical of an underreactor: the façade of pleasantness while you're seething inside, the physical symptoms, and the unwillingness to rock the boat.

Learning to Find the Words

Another classic example of underreaction was demonstrated by Kim, whose father-in-law, Phil, had been sexually aggressive with her.

"So what was I supposed to do? Deck him? I told my husband and I told my mother-in-law . . . "

"But you didn't say anything to Phil, did you?" I asked.

"Like what?" she wondered.

"Well, let's say you've got a teenage daughter. Let's imagine he'd done the same thing to her. Do you think you would have been able to think of some things to say then?"

"Of course I would," Kim answered. "I would have told him that he's a creep and he'd better get some help. I would have told him to stay completely away from her, that if he ever came within three feet of her we would not come over again and that he would never again be welcome in our home. I would have told my husband about it immediately and insisted he lay down the law with his father. I would have told my mother-in-law that she'd better wake up to the kind of man she's married to, and I would've let the other family members know to be especially careful with their kids around him."

"So why couldn't you do that for you?" I asked.

"I don't know. . . . I just got paralyzed. I was so shocked by his behavior, I couldn't think of anything to say. It's hard for me to get angry for me—I can do it for people I love, but somehow it doesn't seem as important when it's me."

Notice Kim's very telling statement: "It doesn't seem as important when it's me." As Diane and Kim both clearly illustrate, people who underreact when they need to take some action usually have a distorted version of their own value and importance in relationship to everyone else. If you're an underreactor, you will:

- Constantly ignore your own feelings
- Believe what's wrong is really all your fault
- Pretend everything is fine when it's not
- Turn your repressed feelings into physical complaints
- Put up with what others do to you rather than start World War III
- Have a history of not knowing how to protect yourself

If you recognize that even one or two of the items on this list describe what you characteristically do with the conflicts that are impairing your well-being, you are an underreactor.

On the surface, underreacting looks healthier than overreacting because you're not creating a lot of uproar. But neither extreme will work for you. Underreaction has a very short-term payoff. It will temporarily delay the time when you do need to take action. But the downside far outweighs the momentary relief. By delaying, you are only allowing everyone's negative behavior patterns to become more firmly entrenched, impairing your self-respect. And keeping up a false façade is emotionally exhausting. I think you will agree that these results are far too costly.

Let the Feelings Out

If you've been underreacting, it's time to take a chance and let your feelings out. Like so many self-defeating behaviors, underreaction has its roots in fear: fear of looking bad, fear of having people disapprove of you, fear that you'll fly out of control. The interesting thing is that the longer you suppress your anger and upsets, the greater the chance that you'll experience just the kind of enormous blow-up that you've been trying so hard to avoid. In my experience, people who shunt all their unexpressed feelings into a volatile reservoir tend to blow much bigger than those who've learned to release their emotions in a safe way.

For an underreactor, there's often a delay between the time something happens—an insult, an affront, an engulfing invitation—and the time you recognize it. You can shorten the lag time, and make yourself more aware of how you're really feeling in the moment, by practicing the "ouch" technique. When you find yourself tensing, your heart pounding or your stomach clenching after an encounter with your in-laws or partner, as soon as you notice those tell-tale signs from your body, stop and review what just happened. Then tell yourself, or even say aloud, "Ouch! That hurt." Resist the automatic urge to push the anger down and forget it. Stay with the feeling. Acknowledge to yourself: I'm angry. I'm hurt. I'm upset. Ouch.

Saying "ouch!" may sound silly, but it's a great way of opening the channel between what your body obviously recognizes in the moment it happens and what your mind acknowledges. You may find that your "Ouch" evolves to "Ouch! That hurt and I deserve better," or "Ouch! That hurt and I'm mad as hell."

You may also want to simply say:

- I feel angry
- That didn't feel good
- I'm upset
- I'm angry and I'm afraid I might explode

Practice first with friends or siblings—people you feel safe with. You deserve the relief you'll feel when you let your true feelings surface, even when it means replacing a safe, false smile with the word "anger."

As you begin to let your feelings surface more quickly, you'll notice a greater sense of urgency building—you'll want to respond when you realize you've been hurt. And with the new communications skills you'll be learning in the next chapters, you will be able to do it effectively.

Once you have digested the work in this chapter, you can move on to look at the part that unrealistic expectations have played in the distress you're feeling.

9

When Expectations Play Havoc

Imagine, just for a moment, that your wedding ceremony had sounded like this:

"Do you ______ take _____ to be your lawful wedded husband/wife? Understanding that as you become part of your partner's family, there may be love and affection, but there will also inevitably be differences and conflicts? Do you also promise to keep your expectations realistic and not project all your needs and fantasies onto your partner or your in-laws? Do you promise to examine those expectations when you feel disappointed, resentful, angry, or hurt?"

Very few people would be able to answer an unqualified "yes" to those questions, which play a sizeable role in most in-law conflicts. So let's take a good, clear-eyed look at unrealistic expectations—what they are and what they do to you.

Trap #4: Unrealistic Expectations of Yourself

You've got a good job, you're strong and healthy, maybe you've got nice kids, nice friends. So you've convinced yourself that anyone who functions as well as you do can handle anything, including those *?*%##!* in-laws. You can take it, you tell yourself. You're an adult (even if no one else in the family is). It's your job to stay cool, endure the bad stuff, and radiate goodness and sanity until everyone else comes to their senses.

Holly, whose mother-in-law, Judy, relentlessly criticized her weight, acknowledged that she had expected much too much of herself in the face of Judy's cruelty.

"You don't know how many times when I was close to tears I told myself, 'You're strong. Don't let her get to you. Don't stoop to her level.' After all, how much can words hurt, right? They're only words. But you know what, they hurt a lot. Then I felt like a real wuss because I couldn't just let them bounce off of me."

Not only did Holly underestimate the power that Judy's words had over her, she also blamed herself for not being able to turn the other cheek.

Holly was strong in many areas of her life, but, unfortunately, good job performance or the ability to work well with other people doesn't automatically mean those same skills will carry over into your family relationships.

I asked Holly to take a look at what she'd expected of herself in her dealings with Judy and bring in a list of her expectations—realistic and unrealistic—for our next session. When she came in the following week, she told me the assignment was a real eye-opener for her:

"Oh, man—did I ever get in touch with how I've been beating up on myself because I couldn't live up to this impossible standard. I realized how unrealistic it's been to expect myself to be superhuman and without normal vulnerabilities with Judy. I know that Preston can hurt me terribly, but I just didn't realize how much Judy could get to me. The most important thing I admitted to myself is that it's realistic to be hurt when you're insulted, it's realistic to get angry when you're attacked, and it's realistic to say 'ouch.' I guess, what I'm saying here is that it's realistic to expect yourself to be a person with feelings, and totally unrealistic to think you're made of iron."

As Holly discovered, no matter how many positive attributes you have, it's almost impossible for anyone to be assaulted by bad treatment and expect to brush it off like so much lint on a collar. And those expectations were preventing Holly from dealing appropriately with Judy. She would learn to get less reactive to criticism and rejection, not by stuffing her hurt feelings, but by dealing directly with the person who was treating her so badly.

What do you expect of yourself when you run into your in-laws' toxic behavior? Is it realistic—or is it superhuman? Would you hold your best friend to the same expectations?

Trap #5: Unrealistic Expectations of Your Partner

Throughout this book, you've met women and men whose partners left home physically but not psychologically. How long did you expect it to take for the marriage bonds to take hold? A year? Two? Nobody has a clue. Most people just expect that once the couple walks away from the ceremony together, they've left their parents behind and become a strong new unit.

Like almost everyone else, you probably assumed that your partner's shift from their parents' orbit to yours would happen automatically and instantaneously—even if you had plenty of warning signs that it was going to be tough for him or her to make the break, just as it may be difficult for you to make the break from your own parents. And most people expect their partners to be protective and to stand up for them when anyone attacks them—no matter what.

Liz, the child-care aide, was deeply hurt when her husband, Paul, framed her mother-in-law Terry's engulfing behavior in very benign terms. Paul even went a step further and made Liz's upset her problem and told her it was the inevitable result of her unhappy childhood.

Liz, of course, could only focus on how betrayed she felt. I suggested that it was a tad unrealistic to think that Paul would suddenly see his mother through Liz's eyes and realize how engulfing she had become. A major shift like that was not going to happen overnight. And it certainly wasn't going to happen if Liz kept making Terry the villain of the piece.

I asked Liz to focus on how Paul viewed his mother and try to put herself in his shoes for a moment. I said to her:

"His mom's behavior is perfectly normal and familiar for him. He perceives it as very benign, and he interprets everything through his own filter. He hasn't yet been able to understand that you don't see through his eyes or that you have different perceptions. The person we marry isn't a clone of us. Paul grew up differently. This is what he has always known. There's no way he's going to grasp the way his parents' demands feel to you. And, unfortunately, like a lot of people, when push comes to shove, he's going to side with the people he's got the longer history with. Sad, but true. I know Paul said he's willing to come in, but if you want him to understand your feelings, you've got to understand his as well, and give him time. In the meantime, try negotiating some compromises with his parents. Barter with them. Go with them for some things in exchange for doing things on your own. That should make things better. And get out of that victim mind-set. There are a lot of solutions to this situation. Plus, you've been so preoccupied with how angry you are, you forget to remember that you've got a nice husband and a job you like—the only thing you're a victim of is your own unrealistic expectations."

Changing the Climate

Pete, the insurance salesman you met in chapter 3, also found that the words "I do" didn't have the alchemy to transform his wife, Ellen, into a wife first and a daughter second.

"Okay, so I fell into what you call 'the unrealistic expectations trap.' How do I get out of it? I thought if I pointed out how her father is so possessive enough times, she'd slap her forehead and go, 'Of course he's doing that. How could I have not seen it? I didn't realize how much this was upsetting you, and I'll ask him to stop calling so much and being so involved in our lives.' Who am I kidding? This is total fantasy."

Pete practically begged me for some specific strategies to help Ellen get unenmeshed from her father right now. I explained to him that there was little that could accomplish that task until Ellen was ready. And even then, it's a process that takes time and a lot of patience. Ellen was simply not able to comprehend why her father's behavior, which she had lived with all her life, was a problem. He coddled her and jumped in whenever she needed anything, so Ellen got to have two men taking care of her.

I told Pete I would bet he got labeled the bad guy every time he complained about Ellen's father.

"Oh yeah—her favorite comments are: 'You're too sensitive, you're too emotional, I don't see any problem, can't you cut him some slack, he's just trying to help.' God, I am so totally pissed. I'm beating my head against the wall. I'm sick and tired of my wife acting like a six-year-old and running to Daddy for every problem she has. What am I? Just a paycheck??"

Pete needed some interim strategies before he sat down with Ellen for a serious attempt to resolve this problem. My hope was that she would agree to come in for some counseling with him, even though, as far as she was concerned, this was all Pete's problem. In the meantime, Pete was about ready to burst.

"Pete," I began. "You said you're beating your head against the wall. All that does, of course, is give you a very bruised and battered head. How about, for the time being, you walk around the wall and stop trying so hard to get Ellen to see things your way? I know what I'm going to ask of you is tough, but yelling louder or sulking longer isn't going to help anything. You've been blowing a trumpet in her ear and you still haven't gotten her attention. So what I'd like you to do now is stop everything you've been doing—arguing, reasoning, trying to get her to see things your way, all that stuff that's frustrating the hell out of you—and do nothing until I've had the chance to teach you some very new ways of responding and expressing yourself.

"You knew what you were getting into. You had all kinds of indications that Ellen was very fused to her father. If you marry someone who puts carrots in their ears, it's pretty unrealistic to expect that they'll suddenly stop the day you get married. Just as it was very unrealistic to believe that Ellen would immediately become an independent, mature woman. So this week I'd like you to sit down quietly and write out as many of your unrealistic expectations about Ellen as you can think of. Then I'd like you to write out what is realistic to expect over time—not overnight. This is part of shifting your focus from what they're doing to you to a new perspective on your situation. In the meantime, I want a commitment from you that you won't talk about Ellen's father with her, if at all possible. If you do, it's in your best interests to be as noncommittal and accepting as possible. That's the climate in which there's a chance for you and Ellen to build a solid base together. Your unrealistic expectations are understandable, but they're a piece of what's creating so much tension, which is going to push Ellen deeper into the comfortable world of her father. No talking about Ellen's dad, deal?"

Pete was truly hungry for some direction and asked if he could have an extra session as soon as he'd finished his list of expectations. I want to share part of that list with you in the hope it will start to shift some of your thinking and attitudes as well:

It's unrealistic to expect:

- That Ellen will automatically put my wishes above her father's.
- That what makes *me* uncomfortable makes *her* uncomfortable.
- That she knows things have to change.
- That she will see her father through my eyes. His behavior is so familiar to her, it's probably invisible.

- That she will be so concerned that I'm upset with her father she'll forget about wanting to please him.
- That she knows how to change.

It's realistic to expect:

- That people will do what they've always done until they have a reason to do something else.
- That I'll have to learn new ways of letting her know how I feel and what I need.
- That it will take time, patience, and work to build a solid marriage.
- That it will take time for Ellen to become less fused with her father.

Pete's list should be very helpful for you in making one of your own. Even though he was extremely frustrated, the tone is understanding and flexible rather than angry and bitter. Certainly, Ellen was stuck in old family patterns and had lost all ability to see her father's behavior clearly. But nagging her about it would only push her further into what was familiar and comfortable to her.

Even if you're furious with your partner, it's helpful to dig deep into your inner resources and put yourself back into the observer role. Then you can see how the unrealistic expectations you came into your marriage with have played a significant role in the disappointment and resentment you've been feeling toward your partner.

Trap #6: Unrealistic Expectations of Your In-Laws

It's only human to want love, acceptance, and generosity from the parents of the person we marry, and to feel bitter disappointment and resentment when those things don't materialize in the way you had imagined. It's interesting to me that people who come into marriage from a basically kind and loving family tend to assume that their in-laws will be the same way because that's what they are used to—they've had little or no experience with any other kind of authority figure. But the opposite doesn't hold true. Through the years, I've found that people who come from troubled families believe their parents were unique. So instead of realizing that their in-laws might well have some of the same hurtful characteristics as their own parents, they often expect their in-laws to be like the fantasy parents they always yearned for.

Maybe you have friends or relatives who have great relationships with their in-laws, and, understandably, you hoped for the same thing. But each combination of people is unique. If your expectations of your particular set of in-laws are unrealistic or based in fantasy, you are setting yourself up for unending frustration and, often, grief.

Expecting to Find a Surrogate Parent

Cal, the contractor, was sure he and his father-in-law, Ray, would be great pals. They had many similar interests and both loved working with their hands. But, soon, Ray became critical and often downright insulting to Cal, and, to make things worse, Karen almost always sided with her father and was insensitive to how hurt Cal was. Everyone brought something to the table that created a less-than-ideal atmosphere. But Cal's unrealistic expectations were a major contribution to his distress:

"I guess everybody's on their best behavior in the beginning—all trying to look like great people and everybody trying to get along, so it was such a shock to me when he started putting down everything I did. Were there warning signs? God, Susan, I don't know. I knew even before we got married that, for Ray, the sun rose and set on Karen, but I thought that was great—I've known a lot of fathers who were really distant. I think my dad was depressed for most of my childhood—all he did was go to work, come home, watch TV, and go to bed. So I see this outgoing, back-slapping guy, and I think, well, maybe I can get some of that attention, too. Well, I got attention all right—ninety-nine percent of it negative."

I certainly can't fault Cal for his hope of a close relationship with Ray. Cal didn't have a crystal ball, and, I'm sure, he wasn't thinking about issues of rivalry and competitiveness. As a result, he was understandably bewildered and disappointed—and furious—when his father-in-law took every opportunity to cut him down and acted far more like a rival than the buddy he expected him to be.

"I never realized how hard it is to give up those expectations. I kept doing the usual bullshit rationalizing—he's under pressure, he didn't mean it, I'll take him out for a couple of beers and tell him what a great guy he is and maybe he'll apologize for how he's been to me. Then we'll go to ball games together—you know the scenario."

It was pretty clear that a lot of Cal's expectations were the result of more than just hoping for a pleasant relationship with his father-in-law. Cal projected onto Ray his need to fill the empty place inside him left by his own distant, uninvolved father. Even after he had enough information to know how threatened Ray felt by him and how much Ray was capable of demeaning him, he realized how fervently he had continued to hang on to his hopes.

Neither Angel nor Devil

Rita, whose mother-in-law, Vivian, looked like the perfect grandmother when Rita had her first child, soon became regularly critical and belittling of Rita's parenting skills.

"She looked so loving in the beginning, but now she's such a know-it-all and she just delights in making me feel inadequate. But she's so damn helpful at the same time, I don't feel I have the right to say anything, so I just stew. I thought she was going to be a friend—now I tighten up as soon as I hear her voice on the phone, because I know I'm going to have to listen to her lectures. I thought she was going to be genuinely helpful—I didn't know I was going to have to pay such a high price."

I pointed out to Rita that she had a potent mixture for trouble here—unrealistic expectations that Vivian would be some kind of Saint Grandma, and Rita's own victim mentality, combined with her unwillingness to speak up.

In working with Rita, I sensed that one key to shifting her perceptions and reactions was to help her find a solid middle ground between the angel/devil extremes she had cloaked Vivian in. Her mother-in-law was neither as flawless as she had first thought nor as malevolent as she thought she was now.

I asked Rita to close her eyes and picture Vivian as she had first imagined her to be—the angel, complete with a white flowing gown and wings. The angel who would make up for all the problems and insecurities Rita had ever had and be the perfect mother/grandmother.

I asked her to tell me what she saw and how it affected her:

"I want her to love me unconditionally. . . ."At that point, she stopped herself. "God—she looks so silly flying around up there. Maybe what I'm realizing is, I don't want her to have any mission in life other than to nurture the baby—and me. I don't want her to have any flaws—I don't want her to have any of her own hang-ups—I don't want her to be human! But she is—with all her good qualities and infuriating ones, she's just a person, not some celestial being."

To further reinforce this shift for Rita, I asked her to picture Vivian as the stereotypical devil, with red suit, pitchfork, and all, the pitchfork pointed right at her.

"She looks even sillier this way—I'm remembering an old Halloween devil costume my brother wore. That didn't make him evil. I guess, when people disappoint us, we make them into devils—I know I do that with Vivian."

"Rita," I said, "you certainly need to set some boundaries with Vivian, and let her know how often it is OK for her to come over, and how to nip the critical stuff when it starts. I'll show you how to do that and withstand the guilt- or obligation-peddling. In the meantime, it will help you to remind yourself that Vivian's smugness and criticism, which, of course, feel awful to you, are a result of her history, just as your sensitivities and expectations and hopes for what kind of relationship you could have with her are a result of yours. People who feel OK about themselves don't need to build themselves up by putting other people down. My guess is, she probably got criticized a lot herself, so this is familiar behavior to her. And, you know—I think you'll get to the point where you can tell her that and maybe learn something about her insecurities. That could create some new intimacy between you and take your relationship to an adult-to-adult level."

Renunciation and Release

In chapter 1, we saw how Leslie trapped herself in an intensifying cycle of longing for more than her in-laws were willing, or able, to give her. Her pain went far beyond disappointment, and, combined with her husband's passivity, it almost destroyed their marriage.

"OK—I know I expected too much, but what I've got is intolerable. Unless they change, and at least treat me better than some mangy dog, I don't think I can hang in there."

I agreed with Leslie that she'd gotten a bad roll of the dice. Her in-laws were often cruel and irrational. But we couldn't do much to change them. What we *could* work on was the pain she was feeling for having to grieve the death of the Fantasy of the Replacement Parents—a fantasy she was set up for, like Cal, because of some major unhappiness with her own parents.

To help her through some of that grieving, I asked her to do a "renunciation ceremony," in which she said goodbye to the expectations that had not served her well.

I put an empty chair in front of Leslie and asked her to put her expectations there. Instead of trying to keep them alive, which was futile, I wanted her to renounce them and let go.

At first Leslie didn't want to do the exercise because it was so painful for her. I encouraged her to try—we could always stop and do it another time if necessary. Little by little, she gathered her courage. At first, she was tearful, but I watched her core strength take over.

"I need to say 'goodbye' to you because you can't survive and it's taking too much energy to try and keep you alive. I don't know why I got so unlucky. I feel so ripped off because I really thought I was going to have a second chance at a new family. But Tommy and I can build our own new family—assuming he shapes up. So I'm showing you the door because you do nothing for me but keep me on a treadmill to nowhere. It hurts—in fact, it sucks big-time, but, I guess, that's the way the cookie crumbles."

I asked Leslie how she was doing. She answered: "I'm feeling sad, naturally, but I'm also feeling a lot of relief knowing I don't have to keep wanting something I just can't have."

At that point she looked at me with a lot of intensity: "I just realized something—I have a lot of work to do with my own parents. I've been so focused on getting my in-laws to love me that I've neglected to pay attention to how much I need to clean up from my childhood. I think when I get some of that handled, I'm going to feel a lot less pressured with Sal and Gina. It's like the lack of love from them was layered onto my problems with my folks, and I just had more than I could handle. I'm feeling sad, but I'm also feeling a lot of relief."

By beginning to renounce her expectations with her in-laws, Leslie had also discovered some profound truths about herself. She had brought a lot of personal unfinished business with her own parents into her marriage, which kept her from being as strong and clear with both Tommy and his parents as she might have been. There is no question that the more baggage we carry, the more we project our yearnings onto other people who, as in Leslie's case, may not have the capacity to give us much at all.

REALISTIC ACCEPTANCE

To further reinforce the renunciation of your unrealistic expectations as you prepare to deal with your partner and then, later, with your in-laws, I suggest that we ground ourselves solidly in reality. Or, to put it another way, as a friend of mine once said, it's time to accept that "what is is, and what ain't ain't."

These are the facts:

You and your in-laws start out as strangers to each other. Your connection to them is indirect, and it forms at first because they have created the person you married. As time goes on, you may form some kind of bond, or even love each other—or you may not. Whatever happens, you cannot change the fact that you have no shared history with them, and you may have very different beliefs, preferences, attitudes, tastes, even language.

They may be people you like to be with a lot, on a limited basis, or would never have chosen to associate with if you had the choice.

Considering all those factors, and as much as you might wish it otherwise, here's an in-law reality check for you:

1. Your in-laws aren't required to love you, like you, or approve of you. If they do, wonderful. But you're not their child, and the bonds they have with you may never be more than tentative.

2. Your in-laws won't change on their own. Tables don't become chairs, and what you see is probably what you'll

get for a long time, or at least until you and your partner take some decisive steps to change the dynamics between all of you.

3. Your in-laws may never become the people you would like them to be, and your blended family may always feel like a rough collage of personalities and temperaments rather than a smoothly woven tapestry.

Realistic acceptance means swallowing hard and understanding these truths. I could see that during the course of the visualization exercise, Rita was starting to move toward a place of realistic acceptance of her mother in-law, who was neither angel nor devil. Leslie, for her part, was considerably relieved that the onus was off of her to find the magic key that would get her in-laws to change. Now she could put her energies toward working with Tommy.

Realistic acceptance has nothing to do with "forgive and forget" but rather with a willingness on your part to end the exhausting and unproductive struggle to get your in-laws to be what you had hoped they would be, to treat you the way you dreamed they would treat you, and then becoming hurt and enraged when they don't.

Toxic in-laws, as we've seen, run the gamut from irritating to malevolent and everything in between. But the unrealistic expectations of "how it was supposed to be" that almost all the people you've met brought into their marriage intensified whatever problems already existed.

PERSPECTIVE TRANSFORMS YOU

You gain a much broader perspective on your situation when you can step back and acknowledge your part in the conflict cycle. This acknowledgment doesn't weaken you in any way or give your in-laws some kind of advantage. It actually puts you in a much stronger position to make your case and negotiate.

As you begin to heal some of the wounds you've been carrying, whether they're fresh or weathered, your self-honesty will enhance your confidence and dignity by taking you out of the defensive, brittle victim stance of "what are they going to do to me next" that so many of us get stuck in. When you're brittle, it's far more likely that you may crack and break. When you're open and reasonable, you can bend with any winds that buffet you.

With new perceptions, awareness, and clarity, plus the realistic acceptance that will replace your unrealistic expectations, you can transform the energy you've been dissipating in conflict and hurt into a calm, assertive approach to expressing yourself, negotiating for change, and finally claiming your rights.

10

Rights and Responsibilities

Read any advice column, or watch or listen to any talk show when the topic is in-law troubles (which it frequently is), and you're likely to hear questions like these:

- Do I have the right to upset everyone?
- Do I have the right to speak up to my in-laws if they hurt me, when they're not my parents?
- Do I have the right to put my husband in the middle between his parents and me?
- Do I have the right to expect my husband to take my side when he's known me for ten years and he's known *them* all his life?

If there are ground rules for our interactions with our in-laws, no one seems to know them, and that makes marrying into a new family very daunting. It's a lot like being turned loose in a foreign country with no idea of the language, customs, or the rules. All too often, there's no guide or advocate—no neutral party who can define what's fair to expect and what's expected of you. Even if you've been married for several years, it may still be difficult for you to be clear about matters of equality, fairness, and defining your rights as an adult.

Complicating matters further, we may tend to see our in-laws as foreboding and formidable. Because they're generally of our own parents' generation, many of us believe they automatically have more rights than we do, and that we don't have permission to protect ourselves, or even disagree, if they're on the attack.

The observational part of the work we did in chapter 9 was one form of the preparation you need to deal with both your partner and in-laws. The self-honesty that comes from examining what role you play in the family drama can only enhance your credibility and strength because you are able to come from a place of clarity and choice. You can step away from the barricades with your mind freed of defensiveness. You're now in the position to clearly see what you are entitled to.

YOUR PERSONAL BILL OF RIGHTS

We've spent a long time looking at what is unrealistic to expect of your in-laws and partner. Now, it's time to focus on what you have the *right* to expect—the basic treatment you deserve as an adult equal in adult relationships—in this complex, entangled group of people, traditions, and emotions. The rights I'm going to spell out for you are fair, they're reasonable, and they're the minimum you are entitled to expect and ask for.

You'll notice that your In-Law Bill of Rights has three sections. Read each of them several times both to yourself and aloud. I want them to become so familiar to you that you'll be able to rely on them during times of stress and uncertainty.

Section I: Your Rights as a Person

You have the right:

- To protect your own physical and emotional health
- To be treated with respect
- To express your own beliefs, feelings, opinions, convictions, values, and traditions.
- To get angry
- To raise your children without interference
- To make mistakes
- To change your mind
- To have time with your own parents, partner, and children, independent of your in-laws
- To be taken seriously

Section II: Your Rights with Your Partner

You have the right:

- To work with your partner to set the guidelines for your household and have them honored

- To ask your partner for help and support with in-law problems
- To protest to your partner when your in-laws are causing you unhappiness or being overly critical, controlling, or otherwise difficult
- To expect your partner to put you first
- To ask your partner to join you in some kind of counseling if things get really bad between you

Section III: Your Rights with Your In-Laws

You have the right:

- To say "no"
- To disagree
- To not love them
- To let them know when they've hurt, offended, or mistreated you
- To ask them to stay out of problems between you and your partner
- To ask for what you would like from them
- To set limits on how much time you spend with them
- To take an active part in the decisions about how the holidays and other special occasions are celebrated

FREEDOM AND COMMON SENSE

Some of these rights are what I call "expectation" rights that need to become part of your mind-set regarding how you are treated. Other items on the list relate to specific behaviors you're going to learn to put into practice when your rights are trampled. These are what I call your "action" rights.

You'll notice that some of the rights contain action verbs like "ask" and "express." These actions will ensure that your basic rights are enforced, and they will guide you toward the new, empowering behaviors that will finally get you unstuck in the in-law wars.

These rights seem obvious, don't they? They are not mean or abusive or malevolent in any way. In fact, they're just basic tenets of human interaction and common sense. Yet many people with toxic in-laws behave as if they were prisoners in a totalitarian country, stripped of all their rights and freedom of choice.

Please learn these rights by heart. Read them aloud several times substituting "I" for "You." Put a copy of them on your bathroom mirror or some place where you will see them regularly. They are the foundation of all the work that we will be doing together in this portion of the book, and the foundation for the positive changes that will take place for you once you learn to put them into action.

EVERYONE RESISTS CHANGE

There's an old Irish saying: "Better the devil you know than the devil you don't know." The comfort of the familiar, even if it isn't working for you, can never be overestimated. What you've done in the past to deal with your in-laws, even though it may be making you more and more unhappy, is known to you. Familiarity may breed contempt, but it also breeds a considerable amount of predictability. You know what to expect and what's expected of you. Change brings with it frightening, uncharted waters—but it also brings a real chance to make your life better.

I know that it's one thing to know your rights in your head and another to push past your fears and ask people to respect them. For most of us, it's very anxiety-producing to know that we're the ones charged with getting the ball rolling. Believe me, you're not alone—everyone is terrified of change, even when our heads know it's for the best. In the many years I have been doing this work, I've learned that as I take people into the unknown world of new behavior, they almost always feel a rush of panic and resistance.

THE FEAR DEMONS

Underlying everyone's resistance to change are deep, often paralyzing fears: fear of abandonment, fear of disapproval, fear of loss. So let's face them head-on. They may not go away completely, but you can quiet them to the point where they're no longer calling the shots.

You've seen Leslie, the young woman who married into the controlling Italian family, permit herself to be treated in a cold and often cruel way by her in-laws, while her husband, Tommy, constantly placated them at her expense.

As I went over her rights with her, I told Leslie, we were moving into the change phase of our work together. When I told her that I was going to prepare her to talk to Tommy and then to her in-laws, she looked incredulous.

"Susan, you're living in a dream world if you think that anything's ever going to change. I can't even imagine doing anything like that—I'm just too scared. And I'm so ashamed of myself for being so scared. You should see me in a work situation—I'm really strong. If anyone else treated me the way Gina and Sal do, I would get them out of my life, but I don't have that choice here—there's too much at stake. They have so much power. Unless, of course, I want to get a divorce and start all over again."

YOU'RE NOT THE ONLY ONE WHO FEELS THIS WAY

What do we do with these fear demons? As we've seen, fear shrinks when it's exposed to light, so taking fears out of our heads and putting them on paper is an easy and effective way to diminish them. I asked Leslie to make a "fear list" of what comes into her head when she thinks about standing up for herself. Here are some of the items on her list:

- I'm too scared to take on all of them
- I can understand why it might work for somebody else, but they're braver than I am
- I won't be able to stand how awful I'll feel
- I'm scared I'll lose everything

I told Leslie her fears were universal, even though she probably believed they were unique to her. Almost all of us tend to look at other people from the outside and think they all have more confidence and courage than we do. We forget that we are comparing our inside world with what we see on the surface of others—note Leslie's comment that other people were braver than she was. Knowing how shaky we feel, it's sometimes hard to remember that behind almost everyone's confident-looking exterior are the same internal fears and insecurities.

To get yourself into a calmer space so that anxiety isn't running your life, I'd like you to make a fear list of your own. Your list may have items like:

- I'm afraid to get angry
- I'm afraid of getting my husband/wife mad at me
- I'm afraid everyone will think I'm mean/crazy/out of control/a bad person

- I'm afraid of my mother- or father-in-law's temper
- I'm afraid of rejection
- I'm afraid of being abandoned

Again, getting your fears down in black and white externalizes and universalizes them, so they are no longer nebulous, shameful presences swirling around inside you. Notice how many of the items on your list keep you stuck in a helpless, "I can't do anything about it" stance. Notice how you have convinced yourself that you couldn't survive emotionally if the important people in your life got upset with you or disapproved of you. Notice, too, how many fears are expressed in catastrophic terms of loss and fear of being left. When your fears are running the show, the adult, cognitive part of you recedes into the background, leaving front and center the child who really did need the goodwill of powerful adults to survive.

You are one of those powerful adults now, and your emotional survival no longer depends on the approval of others. Allowing yourself to be treated badly is much too high a price to pay to keep people from getting upset with you.

SOME CALMING SELF-TALK

I want to give you some fear mantras that I've used for many years with the people I work with. Many of us already have ineffective fear mantras—"I'm afraid," "I can't do it," "It's too hard"—that we play and replay until we feel paralyzed and terrified. I urge you to replace them with the powerful, freeing phrases I'll teach you. You can repeat them whenever you feel the stomach-churning anxiety that is a normal result of knowing that you're going to have to take new and brave steps. Please memorize these few phrases because they will help calm you as you move toward your actual interactions with the people in your personal in-law dilemmas. They will calm you because they are true—and you will feel that truth in the core of your being. Think to yourself, or, if you have the chance, say aloud several times a day:

- Everybody is afraid when they have to do new things
- Everybody is afraid during a time of personal growth
- The fear will diminish as I behave more self-protectively
- Taking action and being afraid are a lot better than staying hostage to my fears
- I have to take the first step while I'm still afraid

Any time you notice your mind slipping into "I can't" and "I'm afraid" mode, stop, take a couple of deep breaths that fill up your belly, and make the active, self-affirming choice to repeat one of these phrases until you feel calm.

Each time you do this, you'll be internalizing and solidifying these truths.

FROM FEAR TO ANGER

The other powerful emotion you need to do some work on before you actually go face-to-face with the people in your life is anger.

Maybe you've known you're angry for quite a while. Maybe you've just realized how angry you are. But one thing is fairly certain: Once you are aware of how badly you've been treated and how much your rights have been ignored, you're likely to find a lot of your fears turning into some pretty intense anger. You may even want to lash out in retaliation. No matter how much self-control it takes, resist the impulse to tear somebody's head off—even though you think they deserve it. That's not the way to get to where we're going.

Remember, rights are not designed to give you license to abuse or attack others, including yourself, but rather to establish the parameters of your position and status in your new family. I know that over the years, like the people in this book, you've seen many of your rights violated time after time by in-laws who won't treat you with respect. And you've probably seen your partner become paralyzed by conflicting loyalties, often allowing your in-laws to ride roughshod over your rights without much protest.

You have every right to be angry. Anger is nothing to be ashamed of. Use your anger as a barometer that something needs to change. Accept it without judgment—it is just an emotion like any other and a very real part of being human.

You may also be frightened of your anger—many people are. They are afraid that, if they express their anger, something terrible will happen to them or someone else. Perhaps you've over- or underreacted. Maybe, like Mara, you tried to deaden your anger with drinking and drugs.

Before you get to the point where you actually state your case to your partner and your in-laws, I'd like you to get more comfortable with your anger and find some healthy ways to start expressing and managing it. What you do with that anger will determine to a large degree how effectively you can reclaim your marriage—and your self-respect.

MANAGING YOUR ANGER

Mara had done some important work on changing her perceptions of her situation. She no longer felt like a helpless victim, and was ready to talk to Rob, but she was still feeling a lot of anger. She was concerned, rightfully, that her anger might burst out just when she was trying to keep things together while she talked to Rob.

Talking about your anger in a thoughtful and nonattacking way is, of course, the goal. Before you get there, however, you may have to do some powerful venting first—but not necessarily to the people you're angry with. The old theories of letting it all hang out and saying everything you feel were popular for a while, but anger often comes out with frightening intensity and insulting name-calling. There are few people who can withstand this sort of assault, and you may do irreparable damage to your relationships.

I suggested to Mara that she let her anger out with me, where it was safe. She had full permission to say everything she'd been holding in, and she didn't have to worry about anyone else's reactions. Since Mara's anger was very close to the surface, all she needed was a little encouragement and she was more than ready:

"First I want to yell at my father-in-law."

"OK," I said. "Close your eyes until you can see him clearly and then go."

I could tell by the changing expression on Mara's face that she was now visualizing her father-in-law. After a few seconds she began:

"You bastard! Who the hell do you think you are, moving everybody around like pawns? You overbearing, miserable shit! How dare you treat your son like an idiot and humiliate him in front of other people? You may have had it your way up to now, you son of a bitch, but no more! You're not going to screw up our lives anymore. In fact, don't count on having Rob working there much longer. How do you like them apples?"

Mara exhaled loudly. "Oh my god. That felt good. It's so great to be able to say these things out loud and not have to worry about the consequences. And I never felt like I was going to lose control."

I told Mara not to expect that one session of venting her anger was going to magically dissipate it. But I told her that she could do this for herself whenever she needed to, when she was by herself. She could use a picture of her father-in-law or whatever evoked his image for her.

It's also extremely helpful to find some purely physical outlets for all that anger. Mara belongs to a gym, so I asked if there was a class that involved kicking or punching movements.

"You mean like my tae-bo class?" she asked.

"Exactly," I said. "That's perfect. Or you can punch a punching bag, or even a pillow at home, when you're alone. It helps to say or think 'No more!' as you pound or kick. And that old line from the movie *Network*, 'I'm mad as hell and I'm not going to take it anymore!' is a good one, too."

Punching, running, gardening, even strenuous housework, like scrubbing, are tried and true outlets for the heightened physical and emotional energy that anger creates. Choose something that gives you a feeling of satisfaction. Smash a tennis ball. Punch bread dough. Throw rocks in a pond. Siphon off that anger so that you're not carrying such a heavy load.

ANGER AND DISCOVERY

I asked Mara if she wanted to yell at Rob, too. She answered that she'd already done too much of that in real life. Then she had a wonderful insight:

"What's really amazing to me is that by getting angry, I

think, I stumbled on a real solution. Rob has to work somewhere else, which won't be any problem because he's really a terrific accountant. But his father's destroying his confidence. I can help him there. That's the answer, and it's been in front of us all the time, but we've been so preoccupied with the problem instead of what we could do about it."

Despite our fear of it, anger can be a conduit that takes you somewhere. Mara's anger led her to a discovery that actually changed her and Rob's life. Even though it was difficult for him, Rob finally agreed that the only way their life could get better was for him to get another position. Mara was able to give Rob the support and encouragement he needed to leave his father's firm and join another, where he was quickly recognized for the fine professional he was.

Resist the Temptation to Beat Up on Yourself

At this point, you may also find that a lot of your anger is actually directed at yourself. New awareness does that to all of us a lot of the time—the "how could I have been such a fool" syndrome.

Al, the insurance broker whose widowed mother-in-law was making his life and his marriage to Julia miserable, briefly fell into this trap.

"I can't believe I've let this go on for so long and just stuffed my feelings to the point where I've almost burst. I'm furious with myself. What's the matter with me? I'm not a weak person, but I have to tell you, I'm really ashamed of myself for not doing something about this sooner. We should have come to counseling a year ago. . . . We should have."

"Al," I interrupted, "should have, would have, could have are the biggest waste of energy. You're here now, and that's what matters. You have nothing to be ashamed of. Let's put that energy into figuring out what you and Julia are going to do about the situation now."

Self-reproach is a very normal but painful reaction to the realization that you've let yourself down. It also is one of our most self-defeating habits. We can't change the past, but we can certainly learn from it so that we can shorten the time it takes for the light to go on.

Catherine, who had become the scapegoat to her in-laws when her musician husband, Sam, turned out to have severe mood swings and was becoming increasingly abusive, sadly but wisely ended her marriage.

But, along with the relief that freedom from her disturbed husband and his collusive parents brought, she was beset with self-reproach.

"I'm a smart person and I'm a strong person. I look back now and I can't believe the things I put up with. I can't believe that I let the three of them convince me the problem was really in me. I didn't know I had the right to define reality for myself. I'm so angry with them, but I'm also furious with myself for letting that happen to me! Who was that woman?"

As Catherine's experience so clearly shows, when you look back on how much you have tolerated and accepted, you may be flooded with disbelief. You may also have a strong sense, as Catherine did, of having lost a part of your true self.

You may also find yourself thinking such things as:

- How could I have been so weak?
- How could I have been so blind?

- How could I have let them get away with so much?
- How could I have let myself be treated that way?
- How could I have been such a coward?

It's essential that you don't beat up on yourself just as you're preparing to get stronger and more assertive. You did what you thought was best with the awareness and the emotional tools you had at the time. Please don't add self-flagellation to the difficult experiences you've been through. Taking good care of yourself right now is essential.

That means making time to do things that make you feel good: getting a massage; participating in sports or other physical activities, including making love; buying yourself something special; meditating; going out to dinner more; going to artistic events you care about. You need to nourish your body, mind, and spirit during this time, and you need to make a commitment to yourself to do so in whatever ways work best for you. This is a far too often overlooked part of the preparation for change. In fact, let's add another right: "You have the right to be very, very kind to yourself when facing a difficult transition in your life."

WHICH RIGHTS WOULD YOU TAKE AWAY?

If you're having trouble accepting the validity of some of your rights, apply them to someone you care about—a friend or one of your children, or a real or imaginary adult child who is getting married. Picture that person in your situation. Imagine that your in-laws are saying or doing some of the hurtful things to them that they've done to you. Which rights would you take away from someone you love? My guess is, none. It's so much easier to see the rights of people we love but it can be tough to claim those rights for ourselves. Yet, once you do, you'll wonder what took you so long.

RIGHTS MEAN RESPONSIBILITIES

It's liberating to imagine how different your relationship with your in-laws might feel if you exercised your rights in dealing with them. But before you get up on a soapbox and proclaim your rights in an indignant manifesto, you need to remember that rights do not exist in limbo. Along with rights, for anyone who is an ethical, caring person, come responsibilities.

I am going to list them now to give you an idea of where we're heading. You'll have plenty of time to examine each responsibility and how to handle it, as we proceed.

You have the responsibility:

- To communicate your concerns and feelings truthfully and without attacking the other person.
- To acknowledge fully what you have discovered you contribute to the ongoing difficulties with your partner and your in-laws.
- To be clear and specific about what you feel and what you want now, rather than going through a long list of grievances from the beginning of recorded history.
- To treat your partner with respect, no matter how angry you may feel.
- To treat your in-laws with respect no matter how angry you may feel.

I know that these responsibilities ask a lot of you, but you have the courage and the strength now to honor them. Before you start to work directly with your partner and your in-laws, you need to internalize what your responsibilities are. This will dramatically increase your odds of being listened to and presenting your case effectively.

11

Grace Under Pressure

"So how do you do all that, Susan?" asked Pat, the makeup artist you met in chapter 2, whose husband, Jeff, would be unpleasant and critical to her after spending time with his parents. "How do you finally say what you've been sitting on for god knows how long, while at the same time not yelling or screaming or crying or getting tongue-tied?"

I told Pat that it's really not all that hard.

There are three techniques that I use regularly to help people find appropriate ways to express and implement their rights through responsible, nonbelligerent communication strategies. They are:

1. Setting boundaries
2. Making clear position statements
3. Nondefensive communication

Let me show you how each of them works to create a positive atmosphere for change. As you'll see, they're exquisitely effective.

SETTING BOUNDARIES

Your boundaries define the nonassailable borders of your emotional and psychological limits. Just as countries have borders, you have boundaries that must not be violated by anyone.

To demonstrate the concept of boundaries when I'm doing seminars or speaking engagements, I ask for a volunteer to come up on stage. I tell that person to imagine I'm someone in their life they're having a problem with. Then I tell them that I'm going to slowly walk toward them and that they should stop me at the point they feel uncomfortable—the point at which I am crossing their personal boundaries.

You can do this exercise with a friend, or you can do it by yourself as a visualization exercise, picturing an in-law who is invasive. I promise you, there will be a point at which you will feel uncomfortable and don't want the other person to come any closer. You can then take that visceral sense of where your limits are into your relationship with your partner and your in-laws—and anyone else in your life who crosses the line with you.

When I did this exercise with Pat during an individual session with her, she was amazed at the clarity of the signals she got from her instincts when I started to move too close to the boundaries of her psychological space.

I told her to hold on to that clarity, and next suggested that she visualize her marriage and her home as a fortress to be protected from invasion at all costs. These were her physical and emotional boundaries—the border between her and the outside world, especially her in-laws. Her job was to find the words that would convey to Jeff just how painful and damaging his "criticism by proxy" felt to her and to clearly set her boundaries and limits in respect to this behavior.

Pat thought for a few moments and then said:

"I want to tell him that this is our home and that it has to be a safe place. I want to tell him that he needs to treat me better, not worse, than he treats everyone else. I want to tell him that he cannot continue to bring all that negativity into our home—that once he crosses that threshold, regardless of what's gone on at his parents', he has to leave it outside the front door—excuse me—the door of the fortress."

What a wonderful and loving way Pat found to draw her line in the sand. Nothing she came up with was attacking or blaming, and there was little that would threaten Jeff or put him on the defensive. In the next chapter, you'll see how effectively Pat was able to help Jeff find the words to tell his parents that he was dramatically altering the "criticism by proxy" ritual.

LAYING OUT THE RULES

Greg, the computer programmer whose alcoholic father-in-law, Vic, came close to injuring their baby, wisely decided to attend sessions of Al-Anon with his wife, Anita, in addition to their work with me. An intervention with Vic, however, did little to change the family dynamic, as Vic continued to deny he was an alcoholic. The young couple knew that they had to set very strict boundaries with Vic. They were working as a team now, and I helped them set some very strict ground rules.

Greg: "I can tell him that we want a relationship with him, but that we will leave if he gets drunk, or ask him to leave if he's at our house. The hard part for Anita is the stuff with the baby, because Vic is so crazy about him, and she knows it's going to hurt his feelings."

"Anita," I said, "your father came very close to hurting your child because he was drunk. Isn't your baby's safety more of a priority than how upset your father may get once you let him know that there are consequences for his behavior? And I know you don't want to hear this, but I think you should be the one, because it is so hard for you to tell him what the boundaries are with Michael. If you're willing to do that, you'll grow ten feet in self-respect."

I asked Anita what kind of boundaries she and Greg had come up with in regard to Vic's being with Michael.

Anita:

"Well, certainly he can't roughhouse with him if he's been drinking. He can only sit quietly with him. And, while I know this will be really insulting to him, I don't think he can be alone with Michael. I guess there should be another adult present at all times."

I complimented Anita and Greg on how well thought-out their limits were, and told them we also needed to rehearse responses to Vic's reaction to their newfound strength. By setting boundaries now, and rehearsing the actual scene until they felt at ease with what they were planning to say, it would be a lot easier when they actually did it, no matter how much anxiety might come up during the real interchange.

POSITION STATEMENTS

When stated clearly and unambiguously, position statements define what you are willing and not willing to accept and what you are willing and unwilling to do. They are a powerful tool in your progress toward empowerment with both your partner and your in-laws. Because so few of us are accustomed to expressing ourselves in this specific and self-defining way, position statements may feel a little awkward to you at first. But like a new pair of shoes that may pinch a little in the beginning, they'll be more comfortable as you take time to break them in and get used to them.

Diane was desperate for some new ways to hold the line with her husband, John, and keep her in-laws staying with them for such long periods of time. I told her that she needed to decide what was OK for her and what wasn't, and then express that to John, and, if necessary, to her in-laws as well. I asked her to say what she was willing and not willing to do.

The first thing she said, was: "I can't have your folks stay with us—it's too hard on me."

I told her that "I can't" makes us sound weak, whereas "I'm not willing" implies choice and decisiveness. "Try the same sentence a few times again," I suggested, "but this time, put 'I'm not willing' in place of 'I can't.' Say it several times. You'll be amazed at how different that sounds and feels."

She did, and she was.

In addition, Diane came up with several other position statements. Here are the main ones:

- I am willing to take the time to find a nice place for them to stay.
- I'm not willing to spend every spare minute we have with them while they're here.
- I am willing to see them several times a week for dinner and a movie. If you need to see them more than that, I'm certainly willing to do some things with friends or the kids.

Diane was somewhat skeptical about how receptive John would be to her new behavior, so I suggested that we find ways to soften what can be rather harsh-sounding statements. There's no need to sound militant to be effective. With position statements, style is almost as important as substance if you want to avoid putting someone on the defensive.

"How about if I sweeten it up a little bit by saying that I know it's hard for him to say 'no' to his folks and I respect that . . . "

"Let me be John for a minute, and practice saying it directly to me," I told Diane. "And if you're not satisfied with how you're saying it the first time around, we have plenty of time for you to practice."

DIANE: Sweetheart, I need to talk to you about this situation with your folks.
SUSAN (as John): Diane—I'm tired and I don't want to talk about this anymore.
DIANE: That sounds familiar. So what do I do now, just nag him?
SUSAN: Let's change roles. I'll be you for a minute. I'm not as emotionally involved, so it's easier for me to think of some things to say to John. It might be a good idea to start by asking him if the time you're approaching him is a good time to talk. If he says "yes," make sure he puts down the paper or turns off the TV and gives you his full attention. If he says "no," ask him to choose a specific time when he will feel more receptive. So let's imagine that time is now. The first thing I would say is something like: "Thanks for agreeing to take this time for something that's really important to me. I know that this situation with your folks has been a tough one for both of us, and I know I've been really unpleasant sometimes because I thought you were not taking seriously enough how difficult it's been for me. I also know that I've put you in the middle a lot, so that it's been a lose-lose situation

for you—somebody's going to be mad at you whatever you do. I want to see if we can work together so that we can both feel better about making some changes. We have a really good relationship and I don't want this situation with your family to spoil that in any way. So here is what I am willing and not willing to do, and then you can tell me the same for yourself."

Diane said that, as John, she felt much less threatened by that approach, but she still had no way of predicting how responsive he would be, considering how guilty his parents were able to make him feel. But she was more than willing to see what happened. I told her that I couldn't predict the outcome either, but I felt safe in predicting that nothing would change until she tried.

Diane realized that these statements, and others like them, were just the beginning, but she was delighted that she now had some new skills to replace her old way of handling the situation—and maybe her migraines as well.

KEEP IT SIMPLE AND SPECIFIC

Position statements are most credible when they're short and specific. Long explanations and vague, generalized wishes only serve to dilute their effect.

The following are *not* position statements:

- I want to be happy
- I want us all to get along
- I want your mother to get off my back
- I wish your father wasn't such a know-it-all
- I can't take any more of this
- I need my space
- We have to work on our relationship

These statements don't impart information that anyone can grab hold of. They're vague, fuzzy, and far too general. No one will know what you mean, let alone what they can do about it.

By way of contrast, here are some other position statements that just might turn the tide for you with your partner and/or your in-laws.

- I'm willing to talk about this with you, but I'm not willing to let you criticize/belittle/demean/insult me.
- My relationship with you is very important to me, but I'm just not willing to bury my own feelings and needs to keep the peace.
- I'm not willing to keep pretending everything is fine when we have some major problems in regard to your parents we need to talk about.
- I'm willing to take responsibility for my role in the problems, but I'm not willing to be told everything that goes wrong is my fault.
- I'm not willing to have your parents interfere with the way we raise our children.

Focus on your position statements to address your particular situation. Take as much time as you need. You know the areas that are no longer tolerable for you. Now define them, put them into clear, concise phrases, and rehearse them as often as you need to until you can say them easily and confidently.

Everyone's position statements will be different. Only you can decide what is and isn't acceptable for you. What will be the same for everyone is that you must find the courage to express those decisions, even if you are feeling shaky or afraid. That's how we grow.

NONDEFENSIVE COMMUNICATION

These skills are the crown jewels of all self-respecting, mature, centered behavior.

Most conflicts follow a pattern of attack, defense, retreat, and escalation—a pattern that leaves everyone frustrated, exhausted, and with little resolved or changed. Nondefensive responses dramatically break that pattern and give you a sense of control you never thought possible. If you've read any of my other books, you know that I use nondefensive responses as one of the major cornerstones in helping people stop arguing, explaining, giving "good reasons," or trying to get others to change their minds. And they're wonderfully simple.

Think over the last unpleasant encounter you had with your in-laws or your partner regarding your in-laws. At some point, someone said something hurtful to you, which immediately stirred the impulse to attack back, argue, or retreat into angry silence (the old fight-or-flight response). You felt the familiar butterflies in your stomach, the tightness in your chest, the increased pounding of your heart. You felt backed into a corner, and your anxiety may have made you go practically brain-dead so that you couldn't think of anything useful to say. You probably spent a lot of time trying to defend your position and show them that they were wrong.

Now imagine that you have a repertoire of responses that you can call on whenever you're under attack and that are almost guaranteed to turn down the heat, restoring your dignity and confidence. They are also almost certain to maneuver the other person into a position where *they* feel off-balance instead of you, and, in most instances, the attack against you will sputter out. Amazingly, you can learn those skills in a very short period of time. I realize these statements sound somewhat grandiose, but I wouldn't make them if I hadn't seen the miracles these strategies have accomplished in my clients' lives—and my own. Let me give you an example:

Steve, the stockbroker you met in chapter 5, was fed up with bailing out Stan, his financially reckless father-in-law, and genuinely motivated to do something about it, but he just didn't know how. Every time Steve tried to say "no" to Stan, both his wife, Andrea, and mother-in-law, Lois, pleaded with him to help out "just this one last time," and Steve ended up giving in.

I asked Steve what he usually did when Stan put the arm on him.

"I tell him that we just don't have the money to spare. I try to suggest that he could get a debt counselor, but he won't hear of it. If I do find the guts to turn him down, he lights into me. He calls me selfish, arrogant, a big shot—anything he can think of. He says I'm callous. He accuses me of not caring if he and Lois lose their home. . . ."

"And what do you do then?" I asked.

"Well, I remind him of all the times I've helped out in the past. I tell him I do care, and that I'm not callous—we just have a lot of bills right now. . . ."

"So you try to defend yourself?" I asked.

"Yeah—for all the good it does. Everybody ends up yelling or crying, and I feel like a turd."

"Steve—getting defensive never does any good. You're such a sweet guy, and you're drowning in all of this. I want to throw you a life preserver. I want you to listen very carefully to this group of nondefensive responses I'm going to demonstrate for you, and then I want you to try them out for yourself."

"Wait," Steve said. "If you don't defend yourself, the other guy will see you as a wet noodle and walk all over you."

"That's a big mistake a lot of people make. The reality is, when you stay calm and nonreactive and don't try to explain or justify yourself, you are far more powerful. Let me show you."

I asked Steve to call me some of the negative names Stan had used and I was going to respond nondefensively.

STEVE (as Stan): You're callous and arrogant.
SUSAN: I'm sure you see it that way.
STEVE (as Stan): Well, I do see it that way and I don't like it.
SUSAN: I'm sorry you're upset.
STEVE (as Stan): So what are you going to do about it?
SUSAN: Nothing. But I am sorry you're upset.
STEVE (as himself): I can't think of anything to say next. I feel like I'm fighting a fog bank.
SUSAN: That's right! That's exactly the point! I took the heat out by refusing to argue or explain, and you had nowhere to go. That's what nondefensiveness can do, and it works ninety-nine percent of the time if you stay with it regardless of what the other person says or does.

ADD THESE TO YOUR REPERTOIRE

Here are some more nondefensive responses you can use the next time you're being attacked or criticized or find yourself in the middle of a donnybrook:

- And you're telling me this because . . . ?
- You're entitled to your opinion.
- I'll have to think about that.
- That's interesting.
- I'll be happy to talk to you about that when you're calmer.
- I'm sorry you don't approve.

These responses are invaluable communication gems that will enhance your ability to hold your own in the face of almost any attack in ways you never imagined possible.

I know I've given you a lot to think about and work on in these four chapters. Take your time. Practice these techniques until you feel OK with them. Expect to feel uncomfortable and anxious for a while because few of us were ever taught that we had the right to set boundaries and express what we will and won't accept. Don't worry about it. Nobody gets it perfect and nobody does this without anxiety.

But I can promise you that the more you put these self-validating behaviors into action the easier they get. The important thing to remember is that you don't wait until you're not afraid before you take the first step. Take that first step and you will *become* less afraid.

12

Enlisting Your Partner as Ally

After all the preparing and rehearsing and observing and reflecting and learning new skills, it's Show Time. You're ready to face your partner, the key player in this drama, and directly but lovingly enlist him or her in the effort to improve your situation.

Some of you may be angry or even disgusted with the lack of courage and support your partners have shown when you expected them to be protective. In addition to the conflicts with your in-laws, many of you have also had to deal with painful feelings of abandonment and betrayal by your partner.

But remember, this is a time of honesty, not harshness or blame. And you need to keep one vital point firmly in mind—those difficult people you're talking about are your partner's parents. Your partner may have complained a lot about them to you, and you may believe that you and your partner share the same opinion of their behavior. Maybe you do.

But, as you've seen, it is one of the great paradoxes of parent-child relationships that most people will defend their parents when those parents are being attacked by someone else. That holds true even if that someone else is you, even if those parents were as toxic as parents as they are as in-laws, and even if those attacks are absolutely justified. If you go on the attack, something very primal gets activated inside your partner and your complaints may sound like a battle cry.

What you say is important, but your ability to get your partner to ally with you also depends a lot on how you say it. In this chapter, I will show you, step by step, how to express the truth of what you're feeling to your partner and ask for what you want. Then I will show you how to deal with your partner's reactions in a way that can dramatically lessen his or her defensiveness and actually strengthen the bond between you.

SETTING THE STAGE

When you deal with serious relationship issues, timing, as in comedy and magic, is everything. To give yourself the best chance to be heard and understood—and to fully take in your partner's responses—pick a time and place where you can have some quiet and calm. Use your common sense. If your partner is stressed out from work or walks in fuming after being stuck in traffic for an hour, wait. The problems with your in-laws aren't going anywhere, and a few hours or even few days aren't going to make much difference. It's not as if your partner isn't aware of how much tension and friction there has been among all of you. It's just that up until now, no one has known how to take the initiative toward any effective resolution.

On the other hand, don't use every excuse you can find to put off this very important step. It's very human to procrastinate about doing something that makes you feel nervous. You may find yourself rationalizing your delays by thinking things like "I don't feel ready," or "We both have too much to do," or "He/she already knows how upset I am. Why do I have to go through it again?," or "Things are a little better right now—I don't want to make any waves." Regardless of how much momentary relief such rationalizations provide, you need to make a promise to yourself that you will open this subject within no more than a week from the time you feel reasonably comfortable with your new communication skills.

You know this person. You live with your partner every day. You know when he or she will be clear-headed and at their most receptive. Maybe you'll want to suggest a long walk as a good way of bringing up this difficult subject. Maybe you'll choose a lazy Sunday morning when you're both in bed reading the newspaper. Do what you can to minimize interruptions. If you have small children, choose a time when they're asleep or with a relative.

There may never be a "perfect moment," so don't wait for it. You both may be very busy people with a lot of demands and stress in your lives. Commit to finding a good enough time in the coming week. I know you're feeling shaky about "doing it right" and how your partner will respond.

But assuming that you're dealing with a reasonable person, I can assure you, as with most major steps we take in life, the anticipation is almost always far worse than the actual doing. You'll feel an enormous amount of self-respect as well as relief when you finally face the issue that's done so much to fray the love and trust between you and your partner.

BRINGING UP THE SUBJECT

This may surprise you, but I urge you to not start with the phrase, "We've got to talk." For most people, these are the four scariest words in the English language. Maybe it's the anticipation that you're going to say something that will make your partner feel guilty, or wrong, or inadequate. You can almost bet that as soon as your husband or wife hears this phrase, they're going to think, "Uh-oh. Here we go again. What am I in for now? Let me out of here." Maybe it's because they hear the echo of so many other confrontations that began with these words and led to a breakup, a major battle, or some other horrendous experience.

Let's try another approach.

WORDS THAT WORK

Calm, quiet, nonthreatening. That's the atmosphere you want to create. Open the doors between yourself and your partner with phrases like:

"Honey, there's something that's troubling me and I really need some time with you. Could we go for a walk?"

"I need your help with something that's been bothering me."

"Is this a good time to sit together and talk about some of the things that are going on in the family?"

Once your partner agrees to give you his or her full attention, you then need to ask them to hear you out without interrupting, assuring them that they will have all the time they need to respond.

I know a lot of this may sound somewhat formal and contrived, but it's just meant to be a framework to guide you toward putting things in your own words.

GETTING TO THE HEART OF YOUR CONCERNS

Now that you have your partner's attention, take a deep breath, take your time, and gather your thoughts. Then start with these four points, which will focus and clarify what's been so troubling for you.

Point 1.	This is what your mother/father do that is very difficult for me
Point 2.	This is how it makes me feel
Point 3.	This is how it affects our relationship
Point 4.	This is what I want from you now

Let's go through this list point by point so that you can avoid the pitfalls that are always present in any emotionally charged exchange.

1. This Is What They Do

This is the easy one, because very little of what you say will come as any great surprise to your partner. He or she is probably all too aware of what has been bothering you, even though he or she may see the situation very differently. Even in those instances where your in-laws are nice to you in front of your partner and then do a number on you when he or she isn't around, you've most likely let your partner know what's going on.

So rather than go through a whole litany of complaints, simply describe, from your point of view, the behavior of your in-laws that most needs to be dealt with. Even though you may have complained numerous times, it's still important to start your move toward change with a calm reiteration of the things that bother you the most.

Of course it's tempting to filibuster when you have the floor, but stick to the core issues and be as specific as you can. As with position statements, keep your complaint short and avoid generalizations.

Here are a few examples of nonspecific complaints:

- Your father is driving me crazy
- Your mother is a total bitch and I can't stand her
- All your parents do is pick on me

Here are some examples of specific ones:

- Your parents demand too much of our time
- Your mother constantly criticizes the way I'm raising our child
- As you know, your parents have rejected me totally and closed me out of the family
- Your father is sexually aggressive with me

Just the Facts, Ma'am

Sarah, the medical assistant whose mother-in-law, Claire, manipulated Sarah and her husband, Devon, with money and a lot of guilt-peddling to spend their precious vacation time with her, told me that the time had come for her to tell Devon that this had to stop and he needed to take her seriously. That was the core issue, and I suggested to Sarah that she stick to that issue and not bring up all the other times Claire had tried to control them, starting with the kind of wedding she wanted them to have. That was in the past. But Claire continued to buy the plane tickets and dangle other financial carrots in front of them to get them to go along with her wishes. None of Claire's behavior was malevolent, but it was intrusive, and it was creating a lot of unnecessary friction in her son's marriage. And Devon felt very guilty if they even suggested they might want to spend their vacation somewhere else.

Sarah and I went through the preparatory steps, and she practiced them with me until she felt confident with her approach. The following week Sarah reported what happened:

"The first thing I said after we found a quiet time and I told him there were some things I needed his help with, was: 'You know that your mom puts a lot of pressure on us every time we are about to take a vacation.' At that point, Devon rolled his eyes and I reminded him of his agreement to hear me out. He said he was sorry, but we'd been through this before. I agreed, but told him that this time was different because together we were going to do some problem-solving, and I wasn't going to piss and moan about the situation."

Sarah said something truly important when she contrasted this focused talk with the numerous times she had cried or sulked or complained when Devon had given in to Claire's demands. This time was different because she was calmly stating her case and asking Devon to work with her toward a solution. She also took responsibility for her own ineffective ways of handling things in the past.

You can also cover Point One by putting a "when" in front of what your in-laws do and use that phrase to make your transition into how it makes you feel. For example, Mark, whose wife, Dana, was trying to rescue her mother from an unhappy marriage, began with "When your mother expects you to be her marriage counselor . . . " If your in-laws have been rejecting, you can start with "When your folks are so cold to me and let me know they don't accept me . . . "

Point One is the opening to get you through the door. Now you're ready for the hard stuff.

2. This Is How It Makes Me Feel

Labeling and expressing feelings is rarely easy, but it's a vital part of establishing true intimacy and of letting your partner know that you don't experience events exactly the way he or she does.

Throughout this book, you've seen partners who seem to have little or no clue to the impact that their parents' behavior has on their wife or husband. Part of that lack of awareness, as we've seen, can be their own blindness to behavior that they grew up with and are used to or may be very defensive about. But their lack of awareness might also stem from the fact that you may have been unable to find the words that can turn the light on for them. As a result, they may assume that it's not such a big deal, and you end up feeling unheard and invalidated.

Feelings can usually be expressed in one or two words. Happy, sad, frustrated, angry, overjoyed, hopeless, hopeful. Many people with in-law problems have told me they feel betrayed by their partner. This is an emotionally charged word to apply to someone you've chosen as a life partner, but letting your husband or wife know what's really going on in your emotional world is one of the most effective ways to be sure your partner understands the seriousness of your in-law problems.

Be sure to keep reinforcing the positive feelings you have

for your partner at the same time, rather than unleashing a seething stream of hostility in the name of "clearing the air."

Most people think they are expressing feelings when they are actually expressing ideas. The following statements are all beliefs and ideas expressed as if they were feelings:

- I feel that you don't pay enough attention to what I want
- I feel that your mother is too overbearing
- I feel that your father belittles you all the time
- I feel that you don't love me anymore

This is the way most people express themselves and think they're "getting their feelings out." But notice that there's no such feeling as "your mother is too overbearing." Nor are there any such feelings as the other ideas expressed in the list. As soon as you put a "that" after "I feel," you've left your emotions and gone into your intellect. There's nothing wrong with that, but look how much the "I feel that" sounds a lot like a repeat of your complaints. This will diminish the clarity and impact of what you're trying to get across: how your in-law wars have made you *feel.* Unless your partner is really insensitive, he or she can understand feelings. They're easy to identify with because they're universal and we all have them. Your feelings can move from your heart and, we hope, touch theirs.

A good way to make sure that you're expressing feelings instead of ideas or beliefs is to work with sentence completions, like "When you don't pay enough attention to what I want it makes me feel . . ." or "When your mother puts me down in front of other people, it makes me feel . . ." That will get you in the habit of accurately identifying your feelings and add enormously to the effectiveness of your communication.

Let's go back to Sarah, because she gives us a good blueprint to follow.

"At first, I thought I had been expressing my feelings. I begged, I screamed, slammed doors, cried. I thought my feelings were as clear as that window over there. I wasn't sure what else I needed to say. But then I realized I was just venting rather than giving him information he could understand. Plus that behavior was turning him off and he stopped listening. So I followed the points and I calmly said I felt resentful, controlled, powerless, and disappointed. This wasn't the way I expected things to be, and we had to figure out a way to get some of the pressure off."

It's fine to vent your feelings to an empty chair, or a trusted friend, or the pages of your journal, but when you are facing your partner and trying to problem-solve, a flood of emotions of any kind is going to make him or her feel overwhelmed and helpless.

3. This Is How It Affects Our Relationship

This is the point that, unlike the first one, may genuinely surprise your partner. Some of you have partners that are very aware of how much conflict with your in-laws is stressing the marriage. But for others of you, part of your husband's or wife's defenses has been to deny or minimize their parents' behavior. Therefore, it's quite likely they will deny and minimize the impact it's having on you. They may have seen you cry or sulk after a particularly nasty encounter with them, or heard you pleading with them to intervene on your behalf, but they still may have chalked that up to your being hypersensitive or making a mountain out of a molehill. If so, they will be pretty oblivious to how stressed the marriage may have gotten. And because your partner has his or her own subjective take on things, your bonds may not feel all that frayed "to them."

For all of these reasons, it's vital to express the seriousness of what's going on and to be sure your partner has heard you accurately. Start by focusing on some of the good things between you, since a little bit of sugar makes the medicine go down more easily, but then go to the truth about your concerns about your marriage. Here are some phrases I've worked out during the course of therapy sessions with some of the people in this book. I think you'll find them useful:

- I love you very much, but I don't think you're aware of how unhappy this situation with your parents is making me.
- We've got some wonderful things in our relationship, but the situation with your parents is eroding them.
- I don't think you're aware of how many times I've seriously considered leaving you because it was the only way I could think of to get away from them. Let's work together to find a better way.
- I love you and I want us to be together, but the way you handle the situation with your parents is causing me to lose a lot of respect for you. I hate feeling this way. Let's work on this together.

The Gentle Approach

Sarah told me, this point really took a lot of thought on her part.

"I have lost a lot of respect for him, but I didn't want to say that in a way that would really wound him. So I really struggled with what to say. What I finally came up with was not as direct as it might have been, but at least I let him know the marriage was suffering, too. I told him: 'You know our marriage is the most precious thing in the world to me and I'll do anything that's within my power to keep it safe. But I get concerned about how your constant capitulation to your mom affects you as well as me—and there doesn't seem to be much I can do about it. If you're scared to say 'no' to her, just remember, I'm here and totally on your side. But sometimes I don't believe you're totally on *my* side, because what I want to do for our vacation takes second place to what your mom wants, and that hurts me and it shakes the trust I have for you."

Sarah wisely and lovingly didn't go after Devon with both barrels blazing and make him feel like a total wimp. Instead, she gently let him know that things had to change, but she enlisted him as an ally and reassured him of her commitment to him. She also stuck to one subject rather than bringing up a laundry list of all the things that Claire had done that upset her.

4. This Is What I Want from You Now

You've thought about what you want from your partner when you were driving to work or lying in bed unable to sleep. "If only he would . . ." "If only she would . . ."—everything would be so much better.

This is probably the most important of the four points. Here you are really asking your partner to take some big steps toward emotional independence and seeing if he or she has the willingness and the capacity to do so.

You need to be very clear on what it is you want, or your partner will be confused. Be realistic and don't overwhelm him or her with demands you know are excessive. Start with one thing your partner can do to improve the situation.

Frame your requests in firm but nonthreatening ways. Here are some examples of how to be both gentle and clear about what you want:

- I would like you to tell them . . . (that remarks like that are not acceptable/we will make our own decisions about how we raise our children/you will not tolerate them being so critical of my appearance).
- I would really appreciate it if you would . . . (try to see things from my point of view/realize that I have a different reaction to them than you do/stop telling me I'm too sensitive when I have a normal reaction to a criticism or an insult).
- It would feel so good to me if you would . . . (stop them when they start to talk about me behind my back/tell me I'm right sometimes/show me that my feelings are at least as important to you as theirs/let them know that we're a team).
- It would really make me feel validated if you would . . . (say that I'm a part of this family and that you and I are a family as well/tell them they're hurting the person you love and if they don't stop there will be consequences).

When you're expressing what you want, it's essential to avoid name-calling and belittling statements like:

- I want you to grow up
- I want you to get some balls
- I want you to stop being such a wuss
- I want you to agree with me how awful they are
- I want you to never see them again unless they stop being so mean to me

PUTTING IT TOGETHER

Sarah started with a position statement that then helped her move gracefully into what she wanted:

"I'm willing to overlook a lot of things Claire has done in the past, but I'm not willing to continually cede over to her the rights to where we spend our vacation. Now we're going to have to deal with this again in a couple of months, so what I want from you is to tell her that we've made plans and we're going to Hawaii. And if she makes a big fuss, which she probably will, I want your assurance that, this time, you're not going to back down."

It may be difficult for some of you to understand how it could be such a big deal to tell your mother you're going to spend your vacation with your wife alone. After all, what Sarah was asking of Devon may seem fairly minimal. But, for Devon, with a history of being the caretaker of his mother's emotional well-being, it wasn't minimal at all. In fact it was the emotional equivalent of asking him to try sky-diving for the first time.

FINDING YOUR BALANCE

It will take time for you to find the balance between expressing your feelings and wants and reassuring your partner that you're having this session because you want to get closer, not pull away. Think about what you want to say, then say it aloud, to a mirror, a photo of your partner, whatever, until the words feel familiar and you can express them with a certain amount of ease. You need to be an artist and to paint your partner a picture in very clear terms that he or she can see easily without becoming defensive.

An important part of your job at this juncture is to avoid

playing therapist or mother, or claiming the moral high ground. One good way to avoid that is by telling your partner you've done a lot of self-reflection and you're willing to take responsibility for your own contributions to the situation. In doing that, you let your partner know that you are willing to be part of a team effort to shift the situation rather than taking the role of a holier-than-thou overseer.

The other key way to show that you want to work with your partner toward change is to listen carefully to how they respond and negotiate. You've opened a two-way channel of communication, and you'll need to pay close attention to what comes back to you.

13

Dealing with Your Partner's Response

In the best of all worlds, your partner is open and supportive, and you'll hear things like:

- I've been miserable about this too. How can we deal with it together?
- I'm so sorry. I didn't realize it was that bad for you. What can I do to help?
- I know I've been putting off dealing with this for far too long. Let's help each other figure out the best approach.

Words like these will, of course, be music to your ears. Now you can think of yourself as a team and give each other the benefit of what you know. You have a whole new set of skills and strategies, and your partner has intimate knowledge of your in-laws.

If your partner is begrudgingly willing, you'll hear phrases like:

- I agree there's a problem, but I don't know what to do about it.
- You're right, but I'm under too much pressure right now to take on my parents.
- You're right—but what about your parents—they're not so perfect, either.

Responses like this indicate that your partner is anxious and apprehensive, which is making him or her feel paralyzed. As a result, your partner is side-stepping and muddying the waters by bringing up other issues in the hope of distracting you. But with encouragement from you, he or she could quite possibly be moved to be more proactive. One of the best things you can do is read this book with your partner. And again, give them time. It would be great, of course, if everybody's partner could work out a lifetime's worth of issues with their parents overnight, but that's simply not in the cards. Change is a process, and what you're looking for is to be sure the process has started.

WHEN YOUR PARTNER IS TOTALLY RESISTANT

These are the statements you're not going to want to hear:

- Under no circumstances will I allow you to upset everybody.
- They're no worse than any other in-laws. You just have to learn to get along with them.
- You're exaggerating again.
- The problem is you—you're overreacting/you're too

sensitive/you had lousy parents so you think everyone else is the same way.

- I don't want to discuss it. If you're unhappy, go do something about it.
- It's your problem, not mine. I get along fine with them.

I know how discouraged the responses in this last group can make you feel, but don't give up. As you know by now, the greater the enmeshment between your partner and his or her parents, the more resistant your partner will be to do anything to upset them. Regardless of where your partner's response falls, remember that the initial reaction may not be the final one. Your partner will need some time to absorb what you're telling him or her, and reactions can shift and change considerably. I've seen people who I was sure were lost causes become far more willing to involve themselves in these problems after a little time had gone by. But no matter how your partner reacts to your new skills, your job is to stand fast and not get manipulated into going back to the status quo.

Note: If you are afraid of your partner's anger and you've been walking on eggs in order to not set him or her off, then that issue needs to be dealt with before any other. If your gut clutches in panic whenever you consider confronting your partner on an important issue, and he or she has a track record of exploding, yelling, or worse, any problems with your in-laws are of secondary concern to taking immediate steps to either improve your relationship or ask yourself why you stay with someone you're afraid of.

FIRMNESS, WITH LOVE

Sarah reported that Devon was quite reluctant at first to go along with what she asked of him. But he was sensitive enough to realize that he couldn't continue to capitulate to his mother's demands without further impairing his marriage.

Nevertheless, he was really resistant to the idea of taking a firm stand with her. At first, he asked Sarah if she would deal with Claire:

"He said he felt like a scared little kid and he was really embarrassed. I put my arms around him and I said, 'I know this will be hard for you, but together we can handle the guilt she puts out there. I know, a lot of people have much worse problems with their in-laws, but this is really important to me, Devon. I need to know that you can be a grown-up with your mom, and I need to know that we're a team.' "

Sarah gently let Devon know she wasn't about to let him off the hook. As a result, despite his anxiety, Devon did tell his mother that they had made other plans for their vacation. As expected, Claire was upset, and she tried everything that had always worked in the past to get him to back down, which was the moment of truth for Devon.

I wanted to hear from Devon how he handled that moment, and I asked Sarah to invite him in for one session.

Devon was somewhat sheepish at first, concerned that I would see him as a total wimp since I had some knowledge of the history of his relationship with his mother. I told him, I was far more interested in where he went from here.

As he told me:

"The first thing I did differently was to call her, instead of waiting for her to call and then feeling so tense when she did.

Just that one thing made me feel more in control. Then, when she got upset, I realized I had to make a choice—to prioritize. For years, I made my mom's wishes top priority, but I knew that if I continued to do that, I would hurt and disappoint the person I love more than anyone in the world. What was the healthy thing to do, I asked myself, and what was the right thing to do? Then I thought, OK, if I upset my mom, she'll get over it. She's got a nice husband now, and her own life—why do I still feel I have to be responsible for making her happy? But if I upset Sarah, it's one more time for the water to wear away at the rock, and I'm not going to risk that. I know Sarah's not going to leave me over this, but I want her to respect me and see me as someone she can count on. Isn't that what marriage is all about? She's always been so solid for me, and, in most other things, I'm solid for her, but with my mom, I'm rice pudding. No, that's wrong—I used to be rice pudding. Sarah taught me some of those nondefensive responses, and when my mother saw she wasn't going to get her way this time, I said, 'I know you're upset, and I'm sorry. Maybe we can see each other over Thanksgiving.' I told her I loved her and I would talk to her soon. Then I had a heart attack—no, I'm kidding, but it was a lot harder for me than I'm making it sound."

Sarah was wise enough to realize that, even though Devon was willing now to take action, it was unrealistic to expect him to breeze through this major behavioral change or to magically acquire dynamite communication skills overnight. So she helped him. It's so important to suggest things that your partner can say to their parents, as Sarah did. You can help your partner enormously by clarifying exactly what it is you'd like them to do and helping them find the words to do it.

I complimented Devon on being so open and loving, and for handling things so well. Obviously, it would be wonderful if everyone's partner was as receptive to change as Devon, but even if they're not, there's still a lot you can do.

SOFT WORDS THAT GET THROUGH

Nancy, the young dean's assistant you met in chapter 6, had a much more extreme situation than Sarah. Nancy had married into a wealthy and prominent family who had cut off their son, Hank, to punish him for choosing a wife they didn't approve of. Nancy wasn't sure what could come of going through the four points with Hank, but nothing else seemed to be working.

Nancy said she'd sat down with Hank, who was very reluctant to open up the subject again, but that she persevered.

"At first, he said he didn't want to talk about it, but I told him that wasn't an option—that we'd been doing that for too long and I wasn't willing to keep ignoring what was a very major problem in our lives. Pretty good, huh?"

I told Nancy that was not pretty good, it was very good. Hanging in there when someone says they don't want to talk about something is not easy. Most people will give up at that point, rather than look like they're badgering if they pursue the subject. But Nancy reminded Hank that he didn't get to make all the rules and that there really was no satisfactory alternative, other than to dig into this mess.

Nancy:

"I started by saying that I knew how much the emotional cutoff by his parents has hurt him, and that as much as he loves me, there's a part of him that blames me for the alienation. . . . I told him, that made me feel hurt and angry, because *they* were responsible for the choice to not see us. I told him that the rejection from his parents was painful and bewildering. I felt like they were punishing me just for being me. But worst of all was his resentment toward me that was affecting our marriage to the point where I often felt like just giving up. Then I said, 'I want you to stop punishing me for them cutting off from us. That means, no more sulking, no slamming doors when someone mentions them, no more angry silences. It's the only way our marriage can have a chance and you can ultimately have a relationship with them. OK?' "

Nancy could have given Hank ultimatums, she could have made threats and demands. Instead, she looked at the reality of the situation and realized that that kind of behavior would only create more tension between them.

GIVING TO GET

Hank told Nancy he knew that things couldn't go on like this—nobody was happy, and nobody was really getting what they wanted. He and his parents were estranged, he knew he was transferring a lot of his hurt and angry feelings on to Nancy, and she was getting a double whammy of punishment and rejection. Hank said, the more he thought about the situation, the more helpless and stuck he felt, but he was certainly open to suggestions. He had no idea how to break through the stalemate.

So Nancy got creative. She designed a scenario in which Hank could spend time with his parents, and Nancy could retain her integrity—no mean feat.

"I told him about an idea I'd been cooking with for quite some time. I said, I'd thought of some solutions that might allow him to have some contact with his parents without involving me. Well, that definitely got his attention. So I said to him, 'Look, we're not joined at the hip. I don't want to be in their presence, and they don't want to be in mine, but that doesn't mean you can't see them on your own—even on a holiday. I would prefer to be with you, but I know you miss having some relationship with your family. I promise I won't punish you for going, if you promise you won't keep punishing me for their rejection.' "

Nancy wisely realized that she could get a lot further with Hank by giving him something in return for his agreement to change his behavior with her. This type of bartering is wonderfully useful in negotiating a difficult situation. Instead of only asking for something, you offer something in return. That way, each party comes out with something of what they want. By approaching Hank with such a sensible solution, Nancy created a climate in which Hank had some choices and was no longer just between a rock and a hard place.

Interestingly enough, Hank did reestablish a tentative relationship with his parents, but after a few weeks, instead of being pleased at the new turn of events, he found himself reacting very negatively to the artificiality of the situation. He was tired of walking on eggs with his parents and was able to see the contrast between Nancy's loving behavior and his parents' rigidity and self-righteousness. He decided on his own that if they continued their rejection of Nancy, his loyalty must lie with her. As a result, he let his folks know that including Nancy was a requirement for any future relationship he would have with them—a requirement that they reluctantly agreed to.

Nancy:

"My husband's grown up a lot in the last few months. He was put into a terrible position. I was, too. But I don't blame him anymore. He's young and sweet and didn't want to hurt anybody's feelings. His attitude toward his parents is very different now because of how they've hurt me. As for me, my illusion and fantasies about ever being accepted by them were finally shattered when Hank was invited to their anniversary party and I wasn't. And guess what? I told Hank I was fine with his going—and he decided not to. We sent them a card signed by both of us and we went out to dinner and had a lovely evening."

Things between Hank and his parents might get better—or they might get worse. There's no way of predicting. But Nancy's in-laws no longer hold all the power. Hank decided what his priorities were and continues to set very specific boundaries with his parents. Hank and Nancy's marriage is much more solid now, and they both have new skills to guide them if it gets off track again.

"STAND BY ME"

Steve's new skills were really put to the test when he told his wife, Andrea, that they had to stop bailing out her financially reckless father. Andrea pleaded, she cried, she told Steve he just couldn't be that "unfeeling," but as difficult as it was, Steve held his ground:

"When she saw that her old ways of getting me to back down just weren't working, she said she realized I meant business this time. She said, 'I just can't deal with him. I just can't. Nothing I've ever said or done has made any difference, and I can't bear to see that hurt look on his face that he gets when he knows I'm upset with him. I don't want to make you feel like you're hung out to dry, but you've got to do this without me. I know myself well enough to know that I'll blow it and probably take out the checkbook right then and there.' So what do I do now?"

I told Steve that it looked as if he would have to talk to

Stan on his own, but that he needed to set certain conditions with Andrea before he did. He needed to ask her for the following commitments:

1. That she would stand by the plan to let Stan know there would be no more bailouts.
2. That she wouldn't sabotage Steve's efforts by saying things to her parents like "This is Steve's idea, not mine," or "I don't know anything about this."
3. That she wouldn't give her parents money behind Steve's back.

Steve:

"She said she knew it was the right and the best thing to do, and she finally agreed to the conditions I asked for. It's really hard for her, but I know that's the best she can do right now and I have to accept that."

As Steve learned, not every partner is going to be able to find the courage you want them to have, even in response to all your hopes and creative thinking and planning. Parent issues run very deep, and so can the fears that go with them. Your requests can touch a raw nerve, and activate anger, or stubbornness, or denial. It probably won't surprise you if this happens—after all, you know quite well where your partner's vulnerabilities lie. If your partner cannot agree to become your active ally in the task of changing your in-laws' role in your lives, it's important to get an agreement from them to not interfere or undermine you as you deal with your in-laws on your own.

REMEMBER THAT YOU'RE STRONG

Anne, the graphic designer you met in chapter 1, found herself in a similar position to Steve. Her husband, Joe, agreed that his mother's caustic remarks and constant sniping were a problem but, for whatever reasons, he basically saw it as Anne's problem and something Anne was perfectly capable of dealing with. When she asked him to talk to his mother with her, he refused:

"There are a lot of moments when I start going into 'poor me' stuff. Why couldn't I have a husband who had enough guts to stand up to his mother? Why do I have to do this alone? But then I did what you said and focused on what was most important to me, which is getting his mother to stop her denigrating criticism. At least Joe has agreed to remain neutral. Would I like him to fight this battle for me? Of course, I would, but he's a great guy in so many ways, and I guess I can look at it as an opportunity to gain some confidence."

The compromise that Anne made was not the rosy ideal, but it turned out to be enough. As I told her:

"You're a big kid, and you really don't need someone else to fight your battles for you. You have all the skills you need to deal with your mother-in-law effectively, and I love that you're turning this into an opportunity instead of a catastrophe."

I know that, like Steve and Anne, you would like a strong ally. But if, after your attempts, you can see that's not going to happen, you can still do what you need to. All you really need to go forward is your partner's assurance that he or she will not pull the rug out from under you after you've confronted your in-laws and set your boundaries and conditions.

HITTING THE WALL

We've seen partner responses that involved a combination of willingness and resistance, but the people we've seen so far all ultimately came through, even if their contribution was small. But what do you do with the partner whose response to your attempts to move things to a healthier plane is a loud, resounding "NO!"?

It should come as no shock that one of the most, if not the most, resistant partners I've ever encountered was Leslie's husband, Tommy:

"Any time he even sensed that I wanted to talk about his parents, he would find three hundred things he absolutely had to do that minute. I could never get him to sit still long enough to start any kind of dialogue. But then something happened where I just couldn't put this off any longer. Gina and Sal accused me of stealing money from the business! Well, that was it. So I brought it up a few nights ago when we were lying in bed after we'd made love. Everything was very mellow and close, so I thought, 'What the hell,' and started with how much I loved him, but how his folks' possessiveness and invasions and the way they constantly insult me were really wrecking things. I started to tell him how that made me feel, but he jumped out of bed, put on his robe, and went in the den to watch TV. I went in and sat down next to him. I told him we can't keep running away from this and that, I was sure, together we could find a solution. But instead of listening to what I had to say, he grabbed my shoulders and said, 'Don't you dare. Don't you dare say anything to them. You'll ruin everything! You're going to cause problems—you're going to make things worse!' "

Tommy's statements made no sense. He and Leslie already had terrible problems, and I wasn't sure how much worse things could get. But they were a clear indication of just how terrified he was. Leslie continued:

"Then he starts the 'They're my parents and I owe them everything' routine. He said, 'You like that white Lexus you got—well, you wouldn't have it without them . . .' 'Tommy,' I said, 'that's ridiculous. I worked very hard for that car and, don't forget we used some of the money I had earned before I met you'—and then I realized I'd let him sidetrack me. Plus, I was arguing and getting defensive."

It's easy to stray from your structured guidelines when things get heated between you. If a discussion turns into an argument, get back on track as soon as you can. But I'm not sure anything Leslie could have said or done at that time would have made any difference. Tommy was the proverbial brick wall that Leslie was running into.

Tough Choices

I told Leslie, she basically had three choices—the same three that everyone in a difficult situation has:

1. She could accept things the way they were and do nothing (except of course, be miserable).
2. She could negotiate for change (which didn't seem to be doing much good).
3. She could end her marriage.

I certainly didn't think that not saying or doing anything and continuing to be assaulted by an intolerable amount of interference and control from Gina and Sal in both their personal and business life was much of an option. I also hoped that she wouldn't have to leave Tommy as the only way to improve her in-law situation. But, more and more, that was beginning to look like a serious option. Negotiation didn't seem to be in the cards, and Tommy's stony unwillingness to even consider another way of dealing with his parents didn't seem to be on the horizon either.

No Time for Games

I would never suggest using the threat of leaving as a way of raising the stakes or manipulating your partner. This is not a game, and what we're talking about here is not a strategy for bullying your partner or trying to gain the upper hand.

But Tommy's behavior left Leslie little choice. Not upsetting his parents had been, and continued to be, his first priority, and no marriage can survive that kind of destructive scenario.

Leslie was getting resonant messages about the tenuous state of her marriage. She met only resistance, refusals to help, and, worst of all, demands that she not try to change the status quo. Finally, and with great sadness, she told Tommy that she was going to file for divorce.

"I remembered the first right on your list—you have the right to protect your physical and emotional health. Well, I've been doing a lousy job of that, but no more. This week I went to a lawyer, I got an apartment, and I moved out. Of course, I was devastated, but I had to save my sanity. If anything was going to change at this point, Tommy would have to be the one to initiate it. He's been calling every night. I told him to expect to be served with papers. He's really miserable. He said they're on him all the time about what an idiot he was to marry me, how my leaving only proves them right—that I'm totally wrong for him and I never fit in. They told him he's got to wear the pants in the family and not take me back.

"Last night I told him I don't want to hear any more of this and to not call again until he was ready to be my husband first and their son second. And I wouldn't even consider moving back unless he agrees to counseling. What would be the point? He'd be on his best behavior for a few days, and then he'd start working fourteen hours a day again, and as soon as Mommy or Daddy wanted him to do something, he'd be right over there, and I'd be out in the cold. No, thanks."

You may decide, as Leslie did, that for your own physical and mental health, you have no choice but to leave a relationship in which your partner, like Tommy, is less frightened of losing you than of upsetting his or her parents. I know how painful such a decision is, and it should only be made after you have tried everything to reach your partner. If you do make it, you need to base your decision on a reasoned look at the cost of remaining in your marriage as it is and the cost of leaving. Only then can you take your next steps with a clear mind and a clear, if heavy, heart.

A Surprising Outcome

Leslie had explored every option and had tried her best to get through to Tommy. A marriage simply can't go forward if one partner stands in the way of attempts to move the relationship to a healthier plane. But human beings are very unpredictable, and sometimes the person you are convinced is unreachable and unchangeable can surprise you.

Leslie's courage and self-protective actions served as the catalyst to open Tommy's mind and heart:

"He called and said that he didn't realize how precious I

was to him until he lost me. He said he'd never felt such despair in his life. He said he felt like an idiot, and he hoped it wasn't too late. He swore that things would be different and that he was ready to come to counseling with me if that was OK with me."

Everything Tommy said pointed to a very hopeful outcome if his actions followed his words. I told Leslie that I would see them together for a few sessions, to deal with the immediate crisis, but then I would refer Tommy to a colleague, because he had so much of his separate work to do. That would also give me the chance to keep helping Leslie to get stronger and deal with some of her parental issues as well.

And guess what? To our astonishment, after about two months of counseling, all on his own, Tommy decided to open his own business and to take at least a year's hiatus from any contact with his parents. The last I heard, both the new business and the marriage are doing fine.

WHEN LEAVING IS THE BEST OPTION

Obviously, not everyone's partner will respond the way Tommy did, and not every marriage is strong enough to withstand the major assaults on its stability. In fact, sometimes your threatening to leave, or leaving, will actually cause your partner to ally even more intensely with his or her parents. Your in-laws may take the route of Tommy's parents and use your actions as proof that you are unworthy or unstable—and get your partner to agree, projecting the blame for what has happenend almost entirely on you.

If this is your situation, please do not frame this as your failure. If your situation is intolerable, if you've done everything you could, and used the tools I've given you, and nothing moves, then it is your partner and your in-laws who have failed, and your leaving is probably the healthiest thing you can do.

A marriage depends on both partners' willingness to confront and work through serious problems. You cannot save a marriage by yourself. Most of you will find that your partner will offer something, if not everything you'd like, toward the goal of improving things with your in-laws. It can be a gesture as seemingly simple as saying they will take you seriously and are willing to step aside as you single-handedly deal with their parents.

THE IMPORTANCE OF HISTORY

One great contribution your partner can make is to tell you what he or she knows about their parents. As you saw with Holly and Preston, family history can yield a gold mine of information and understanding. Learning more about your in-laws as people can accomplish several things: It will reinforce for you that what they're doing has little or nothing to do with you, and it will create some awareness in your partner that his or her parent's behavior is based not so much on what they claim to be upset about, but far more on what has never been resolved in their own lives. This, in turn, will make them more vulnerable, human, and less threatening, as you prepare to face them, either with your partner or by yourself.

14

The Final Step

Your in-laws have created serious difficulties in your life, and, as a last step in this process, you'll want to tell them that directly. There are, of course, many different scenarios. Some of you will have your partner by your side as you do most of the talking. Others of you have partners who are willing to take the lead in facing their parents. You may set up a specific time to talk to them, or you may confront them spontaneously, the moment something happens that you need to respond to. Some of you have in-laws who are more annoying than destructive, and others of you have in-laws whose behavior threatens the very foundation of your marriage.

But one thing is true for all of you. You are no longer at a disadvantage. The time when you didn't know what to say and you didn't know what to do is behind you. I know you still feel somewhat shaky about stepping out of your old patterns and taking on people who seemed to have so much power over your life. But you know from the work you've done up to now that just beyond the fear lies positive change.

THEY MAY SURPRISE YOU

In all likelihood, your in-laws see you as less mature, wise, and experienced than they are, and may believe that you have nothing important to say. As hard as it may be, treat them courteously anyway—you can lead by example. Focus on the aspects of their behavior that affect you, not their personalities, beliefs, politics, tastes, or behaviors that don't violate your rights.

Skeptical as you may be of this possibility, leave room for your in-laws to surprise you in a positive way. Some of you will have in-laws that are quite young—maybe just a generation removed from you. And even if they are older, they still may be educated, highly skilled, intelligent, and sophisticated, not at all like the cartoon stereotypes which, for the most part, are very out of date. They may be more open than you think. Of course, that won't be true for all of them, but there's no way of knowing until you take the risk of letting them know what your feelings and wishes are.

THE NONMALICIOUS IN-LAWS

In dealing with the more benign in-law problems, resolve to respond the next time one comes up. When you hear words that signal another round of the behavior that upsets you, take a deep breath and point out the person's behavior to them. Tell them how it makes you feel and ask them to stop. Prepare a simple script you can use at the time the problem behavior arises. Use your position statements, boundary-setting, and nondefensive responses.

Then repeat as necessary. Use your new communication skills as often as you need to. It may take several tries to set a change in motion, but be persistent. It doesn't take a lot of unasked-for advice, negative comments, or sniping to create a significant amount of tension between you and your in-laws. And, happily, it often doesn't take a lot to stop it.

OFFER AN OUT

Rita, who was deluged with unsolicited advice and criticism from her mother-in-law, Vivian, after she had her first baby, had already come to the conclusion that Vivian was irritating but not vicious. She decided to respond to Vivian in a new way the next time Vivian was critical. Rita reported what happened:

"At first, I was going to say, 'When I want your advice, I'll ask for it,' but I realized there was a better way to do it. I remembered the things we'd worked on, and I also remembered some lines from an old assertion-training class I took. The other day, she was over and started to show me some articles about the benefits of nursing. So I said, 'Vivian, you may not be aware of it, but you're giving me a lot of unasked-for advice that feels a lot like criticism to me.' "

Rita made an excellent start. By acknowledging that Vivian was probably not even aware of how hurtful many of her "casual" remarks were, she was being generous instead of blaming. She was offering Vivian an out instead of encouraging a denial like "I don't do that."

Many of the less malicious in-laws may not be fully aware of the effect their comments have on you, especially if you've never been able to say "ouch." Look candidly at the situation.

Ask yourself, "Is the behavior habitual?" For example, are you dealing with a chronic critic, a know-it-all, or an engulfing matriarch who makes unreasonable demands on your time? If the bothersome behavior seems more thoughtless or self-centered than calculated to hurt you, pointing out the behavior and setting your boundaries may be all you need. Just as a fly swatter, not a canon, is enough to deal with a mosquito, with a gentle intervention like Rita's, you can probably clear up a lot of the situation either quickly or over time.

You can also use lines like:

- I'm grateful for your help but it doesn't make up for the criticism or the negative comments.
- Dad, there's that unsolicited advice again. Remember, you agreed to cool it.
- Mom, it's nice of you to always include us, but we have other plans for the weekend.

DON'T BE AFRAID TO BE HUMAN

After calling Vivian on what she'd been doing, Rita went on to do something very courageous:

"I said, 'Look, I'm shaky enough with my parenting as it is, and all your criticism does is make me feel more inadequate.' That was really hard to say because I wasn't sure I should show her how vulnerable I am. But, I decided, one of us had to open up. I said, 'I know you're an old hand at this, but I'd really appreciate it if you could wait until I ask to give me advice.' "

I want to stress again that, in most cases, you will not put yourself in a one-down position by revealing some of your own fears or insecurities to an in-law—especially someone like Vivian. By letting Vivian see some of her vulnerabilities, Rita opened the door to a new level of communication between the two women. There's no guarantee that your in-laws will walk through that door, but if you don't give them the opportunity, your relationship may be doomed to façade meeting façade, without ever making genuine contact.

And Vivian did, indeed, come through Rita's opening:

"At first, she bristled a bit, and I got the usual, 'I'm only trying to help,' but then she stopped, and sighed, and said, 'I saw you struggling, and I thought you didn't have to reinvent the wheel—I wanted to make things easier for you, and, I guess, all I did was screw things up. I vowed I wouldn't be a meddling know-it-all, and, it seems, that's just what I became.' I thought that was pretty great. I know it won't be perfect, but, at least, I don't feel so tense around her and—who knows?—I might even ask her for her opinion one of these days."

DECIDING WHAT NEEDS TO BE DONE

Vivian responded maturely to Rita's gentle confrontation, and it wasn't at all necessary for Rita to structure a formal meeting with a lot of ground rules. I wish everyone could be so fortunate. But, clearly, a large number of toxic in-laws do not fall into the category of "irritating but benign."

The more difficult your in-laws are, and the more critical your situation has become, the more important it is to set up an appropriate time and place for your session with them. You'll want to ensure, as much as you can, that you'll have the benefit of all the clarity, focus, and support you can create.

If you have decided that a more structured session is in order, here are some guidelines to help make yourself as comfortable as possible, and to do as much as you can to ensure that you will be listened to and, hopefully, heard.

ESTABLISHING THE RIGHT ATMOSPHERE

1. Don't try to have this conversation on the phone. Telephones are impersonal, and you'll want to take in your in-laws' nonverbal communication as well as their words. Phones also offer an easy escape hatch. Should your in-laws become agitated and not want to hear you out, they can simply hang up on you, leaving tensions heightened and nothing resolved.

2. Don't meet them in a public place, like a restaurant. There are too many distractions and interruptions, and should voices rise or tempers flare, you'll feel awkward and responsible for making a scene.

3. Do meet them on your own turf, when possible. You make a significant statement about your independence and autonomy by setting your meeting in your home or apartment, among the belongings that reflect the life you've created. If you live out of town and do this when you're visiting them, arrange to have them come to your hotel.

4. Do be clear about the kinds of changes you're asking of your in-laws and use your position statements, boundary-setting, and nondefensive communication skills to let them know specifically what is troubling you. Stick to your script, no matter what kind of negative responses may come your way.

5. Do arrange to send young children to a sitter or relative, and turn off the phones.

MAKING THE INVITATION

Having your partner's active support will, of course, make it much easier to approach your in-laws. It doesn't matter which of you steps to the fore, though that's something you might want to agree on in advance. Your partner may believe that it's important for him or her to initiate the meeting and do most of the talking. Or you may decide that you're the one to get the ball rolling.

Once you've decided that you need to arrange a meeting with your in-laws, here is a good way to extend the invitation:

"I/we need to talk to you about some things and I'd/we'd like to know when it would be convenient for you to come over."

If they ask what it's about or press you to give them some details, tell them that you've given this a lot of thought, and that, you believe, a face-to-face meeting will accomplish a lot more. Keep your tone calm and nonthreatening, and emphasize that this meeting is important and means a lot to you and your partner. If your partner is willing to make the first approach, all the better.

If your partner (or you) are too apprehensive to set up a face-to-face meeting, a letter is often an excellent solution. Letters are particularly useful (not to mention safer) with volatile or abusive in-laws. Letters can't be interrupted, and you can't walk out on them. Letters are also an excellent way to focus and hone exactly what you want to say. You can each write a separate letter, or you can write one from both of you, reinforcing the concept that you're in this as a team.

PUTTING AN END TO "DIVIDE AND CONQUER"

Pat, the makeup artist whose husband, Jeff, had been roped into carrying his parents' criticism home to her, had already started the change process by letting Jeff know that it was time to put an end to her in-laws' "divide and conquer" strategy. She said many of the things to Jeff she had worked out with me.

Jeff understood that Pat was committed to no longer accepting the criticism by proxy and that he could either stand by her side or let her face his parents on her own. Pat's courage was a splash of cold water for Jeff. He woke up to how much influence his parents still had over his life and how he had been allowing them to erode what could be a great marriage.

As a result, Jeff was the one who initiated the call and invited his parents over one evening. When his parents wanted to know what this was all about, Jeff took the lead:

"Mom and Dad, there's something I need to say to you, and I would appreciate it if you would not interrupt me. This isn't easy for any of us, but it's long overdue. I know that you try to be nice to Pat when you're with her, and I appreciate that, but I want you to know that I'm not willing to listen to you say such negative things about her when she's not around. You seem to forget that you're talking about the woman I love, and after a weekend of listening to you criticize and complain, I go home and act like a jerk. So here's what we've decided: no more family get-togethers where she's not there, and if she can't or doesn't want to come for some reason, I'm going to leave if you start attacking her. I want to have a close relationship with you, but you're making it impossible with your behavior."

Jeff said that there was dead silence, as if his parents couldn't believe that their compliant "good boy" had actually told them he was upset with them. So, true to form, they assumed that Pat must be behind all of this and turned what Jeff had said into a justification for renewing their harsh criticism of Pat.

As Pat reported:

"Well, all the phony veneer of sweetness and light that they used to show to my face disappeared, and they took turns seeing who could tear into me the most. But what was so interesting is that they were still talking through Jeff. Mary said to him, 'She's turning you against us,' and Gil jumped in with, 'She's never liked us—she's always been unpleasant to us.' At that point, I decided I had to deal with some of this myself or they'd continue to act as if I was invisible. So I said:

" 'You know, I'm right here, and I'd really appreciate it if you would talk to me directly if something bothers you instead of going through Jeff. It puts him in a terrible position. If I do something that bothers you, tell me. I'm a big girl—I can handle it. But you have to stop making Jeff your messenger. Look, I know we've gotten off to a rough start, but I'm only willing to accept fifty percent of the responsibility for the friction. Are you willing to accept the other half? Why don't we call it a night and you go home and think about it.' "

DON'T EXPECT MIRACLES

There were no miracles. Mary and Gil didn't suddenly turn into model in-laws after that evening, but it didn't matter. Jeff held true to his commitment to leave if his parents began chipping away at Pat. By doing so, he taught his parents what he would and wouldn't accept, and, slowly, they began to realize that there were now some very unpleasant consequences to their sniping. Little by little, they were able to make some adjustments in their behavior—and when they slipped back, both Jeff and Pat called them on it.

If Jeff's parents didn't have the capacity to make major changes, it was obvious that Pat and Jeff did. Having Jeff's active support made it much easier for Pat to speak up. The couple made enormous strides in self-respect, their ability to express themselves clearly and nondefensively, and, most of all, in getting their priorities and loyalties straight. The truly loving behavior they showed toward each other in front of Jeff's parents strengthened their marriage immeasurably.

STEPPING OUT OF THE MIDDLE

Mel and Jenna, whom you met in chapter 5, had the unique situation of in-laws who were far more civil to their child's partner than they were to their own child, whom they continued to abuse and attack. The couple decided that a letter was the best solution for them. After Mel and I had done some work together, he told Jenna that he was no longer willing to serve as a buffer between her and her abusive parents. His in-laws had tried to use him as a conduit to continue to assault Jenna and to make both their lives miserable.

But, as is so often the case, when you set your boundaries, and your marriage is basically solid, drawing a line can often serve as a catalyst for your partner to wake up to just how unhealthy the situation has been. Jenna took some time to think over what Mel had said, and, to his surprise and delight, she finally agreed to get some long overdue counseling to help free her from her traumatic childhood.

"I told her I knew that she was feeling very raw and

vulnerable because she'd just begun dealing with her childhood. I said if she didn't want to talk to them on the phone that was fine with me, but I wasn't going to run interference any more because she's got this cockamamie fantasy that some day she's going to have these great, loving parents. We started screening our calls, but that was only a Band-Aid on the problem, and we were just avoiding things rather than facing up to them. So, I suggested we write a letter together. That felt better to her, but we'd like you to help us with it."

Here are some excerpts from Mel and Jenna's letter:

Mom and Dad: (Jenna said starting with "Dear" felt hypocritical to her at this time)

We are writing this letter together to let you know that things must change between us. Neither of us will any longer accept your angry, abusive phone calls, and if you become nasty, whoever answers the phone will hang up. Now, here are some separate requirements from each of us—Mel first.

To my in-laws:

There are some nonnegotiable limits that I am setting on our relationship. I will no longer listen to you berate your daughter, my wife, over the phone or in person. I will no longer listen to you blame her for your unhappy marriage. From my point of view, you don't deserve a daughter like Jen. But I realize that she still has strong feelings for you and a lot of unfinished business with you that needs to be worked out. I'm putting you on notice that I'm stepping out of the middle and I'm not carrying any more messages for you. I think you were terrible parents, and I wouldn't even dwell on the past if you treated her lovingly now, but I'm through pretending for Jenna's sake. I am, however, willing to treat you courteously for Jenna's sake. At the very least, you owe her a sincere and full apology followed by some kind of reparations. Anything less will just keep the status quo. Paying for her counseling would be a good start. I doubt that any of these things will happen, but at least I'm finally saying some of things I've held in for a long time. If you want any relationship with Jenna and me and your future grandchildren, you need to meet us at least halfway.

With hope,

Mel

Then it was Jenna's turn:

Mom and Dad:

I hope the time will come when we can discuss the events of my childhood and the way you treat me now truthfully, instead of my being so frightened of getting you upset with me. Mel is giving me the kind of support and validation I always dreamed of getting from you, and I'm very fortunate to have found someone who accepts me and loves me with all my hang-ups and fears. I would like to arrange a meeting between the four of us, or you might agree to come in and see my therapist with me. Yes, I'm in therapy—I know you don't approve but it's the smartest thing I ever did, aside from marrying Mel, of course. If I see that you are willing to acknowledge some of the terrible things you did to me in the past and to take responsibility for them, we may be able to build a new relationship. If not, then we will have to have a very superficial and minimal relationship, or perhaps none at all. The ball is in your court. I do love you both despite everything, but I need some evidence that you feel the same about me, and so far I haven't gotten much. I truly hope that can change.

Jenna

Mel became a true warrior, protecting his wife and willing to say many of the things to his in-laws that had needed to be said for a long time. But the biggest surprise was Jenna, who seemed to absorb some of Mel's determination and strength and transform it into her own.

NO ANSWER IS THE LOUDEST ANSWER OF ALL

After several weeks, Mel told me:

"Well, we haven't gotten an answer. No letter, no phone call, no nothing."

"But you have gotten an answer," I said. "The answer is that they're not ready to deal with any of this right now, and they're not willing to accept your ground rules, none of which were harsh or unreasonable. Maybe later, maybe not. What if they never get in touch with you—how will Jenna be with that?"

"Well," Mel answered, "I want to bring her in next time so you can see her for yourself—it's as if she got this one-thousand-pound weight off her shoulders—she's really flowering. The therapist you referred her to is working wonders with her. She's a lot less depressed, and the strength I saw when I first met her is really coming back. I think she'll be fine even if they make the choice that holding on to their self-righteous martyrdom is more important than a relationship with their daughter. That's their choice and their loss. They need us a lot more than we need them!"

And what a sad and bitter choice it was. Nobody can predict what changes, if any, time will bring in Mel and Jenna's situation with her parents. Maybe they will mellow, and maybe they will harden their position even more. There's no way of knowing. But Mel and Jenna are no longer buffeted by cruel and insulting phone calls, and Mel now has a wife who is tending to her wounds and becoming stronger each day. They are truly free.

UNCOVERING DEEPER PROBLEMS

Your in-laws' immediate reaction is not always the final test of whether or not things can get better. Look what happened to Steve.

At his therapy session, Steve reported that during the previous week, he and Andrea had gotten one of their regular emergency phone calls from Stan, asking them to come over to "discuss a small problem." Steve knew what that meant, and told Andrea he was going to have her parents come to their house instead of the usual routine of Steve and Andrea going to them. Andrea was extremely anxious because she knew that Steve had made a decision from which there was no turning back. Steve reminded her of her agreement to not undermine him, and she repeated her agreement.

"Well, the 'small problem' was a foreclosure notice on the house, because they've skipped several mortgage payments. My heart was racing and my stomach was knotting up, so I took a deep breath and remembered that you have to take the first step while you're still afraid. You didn't tell me it would be this tough! But I plowed ahead. I said, 'Not this time, Stan. You've got time on this to consult a debt counselor, and I'll be willing to help you find somebody, but you need to turn things over to a pro and make some plans for consolidating your debts and assets and arranging things with your creditors. But whatever you decide to do, as of tonight, the Bank of Steve is closed.' "

"My God, Steve," I said. "What an enormous leap for you. I'm dying to know what happened."

"Well, Stan turned white, then he turned purple. Lois just

sat there, as usual, shaking her head. Then Andrea did something that meant a lot to me. She moved closer to me on the sofa, which said more than any words could say about her support. Then Stan went on a tirade. He called me selfish, arrogant, a big shot—anything he could think of to paint me as the villain. He accused me of not caring if he and my mother-in-law lost their house or couldn't put food on the table. Somehow he twisted it around so it would be all my fault. Stan asked Andrea how she could be a party to this. I think that's when she finally saw just how infantile and unreasonable they were. She said, 'Dad—you're behaving like a child. Have you forgotten all the times we bailed you out in the past to our own detriment? How about a little gratitude instead of this what-have-you-done-for-me-lately? I'm sorry, but I support him totally and I agree with everything he's said. It's time to start solving your own problems!' Boy, did it feel terrific to have her say that!"

Initially, Andrea's physical presence and silent support would certainly have been enough to allow her and Steve to go forward with their relationship. But Andrea found her voice when her father started playing victim and attacking Steve.

Steve and Andrea withstood the anger, the pleading, and the guilt-peddling. They held their ground. I continued to see Stan and Andrea to reinforce this important change in their relationship to Andrea's parents and each other, and we began to head toward termination of their sessions since their major crisis had been handled. About three weeks after the confrontation with his in-laws, Steve had some very interesting things to report:

"Once Stan saw I meant business, he went into a major depression. He stayed in his pajamas all day, staring at the TV, and wouldn't talk to anybody. Which was the best thing that could have happened, because it finally got Lois off her butt to get him to a doctor. The physician referred him to a psychiatrist, and Stan refused to go, and Lois just said, 'You're going and I don't want to hear any more about it.' Well, the psychiatrist determined that Stan was manic-depressive, and Lois told us he said that much of the speculation and risky deals he got involved with was his way of acting out the grandiosity and the pressure of the manic episodes. He put Stan on lithium, which is leveling out his mood swings a lot. He agreed to go to a debt counselor, and he's much calmer. Andy and I may even be able to have a reasonable relationship with him."

By finding the courage to hold fast even though they knew how frightened and upset their new behavior made Stan and Lois feel, Steve and Andrea set into motion an extraordinary chain of events that culminated in a dramatic change for both couples. Steve gained immeasurable self-respect, Andrea made the healthy choice as to where her loyalty and support needed to be, and her parents regained nothing less than their lives.

THE NEEDY IN-LAW

One of the most difficult ethical and emotional issues anyone has to face is deciding where the balance lies between helping in-laws who are in need, particularly those in fragile physical or emotional health, and maintaining the autonomy to support your own health and the stability of your marriage. You saw this dilemma played out in chapter 4 with Al's widowed mother-in-law, Molly, who had decided that only her daughter Julia could take care of her. As a result, Al felt resentful and neglected, and Julia felt she was drowning in a sea of obligation and demands.

In Al and Julia's case, Molly was financially and physically capable of starting a new life for herself, but had become emotionally paralyzed after her husband's death. I suggested to Julia that giving that exhausts your own financial, physical, and emotional reserves is a sure way to create resentment and tensions that damage you, your marriage, and even the person you're trying to help.

"So, what am I supposed to do?" asked Julia. "I can't abandon her, and I can't stand my guilt when I tell her I'm going to look for a companion for her and she says things like, 'I might as well die—nobody cares about me.' "

"That is such bullshit!" Al interjected. "She says, 'Jump,' and you say 'How high.' And what's ridiculous is she's only sixty-two—she's got money, she's physically OK, she can drive. But I'm telling you, the way things are now, I'm tearing out what hair I have left, Julie—she's got the resources to provide for her own care. She could get a nice live-in companion, or she could go to a nice retirement community where she'll be with people her own age and have a lot of structured activities. See—Julia's always been the one everybody turned to in the family. Her sisters won't do a damn thing for Molly, so everything's always on Julia. But Julia has a husband and kids, and we're really getting the short end of the stick. Molly's lucky—she has a lot of options, which a whole lot of other people in her position don't have. And if you can't talk to her, believe me, I can."

A DIFFERENT KIND OF TOUGH LOVE

Julia squirmed and grimaced, but finally agreed that they would both talk to her. They told Molly that she had several choices, but to have Julia as her primary caretaker was no longer one of them. As expected, Molly cried, she threatened, she manipulated, she refused to consider a live-in, and nothing seemed resolved. Julia felt horrible, but she didn't rush over to her mother's every day that week. Instead, she checked in with her on the phone, and if Molly needed something, Julia suggested she have it delivered. About two weeks later, Molly said she'd seen an ad for a retirement community that looked pleasant, and would Julia and Al drive her there and check it out with her.

Molly sold her house, and Al and Julia helped her move into the new community. Molly is now a member of the residents' board of the organization, she has made new friends, and, at last report, was planning a trip to Mexico with other residents.

We've heard a lot over the years about tough love for youngsters who are out of control. But Al and Julia use many of the same concepts with Molly. They let her know it was sink-or-swim time and that she was perfectly capable of making a new life for herself.

None of the positive changes in Molly's life would have taken place if Al hadn't expressed his insistence at changing their situation and if Julia had continued to allow her mother to stay totally dependent on her. When you first set your boundaries with a needy person you may feel terribly uncomfortable and guilty—as if you're doing something cruel and heartless. But with a needy in-law who is capable, you are actually being kind and loving by refusing to enable them to stay infantile.

LOOK FOR HELP FIRST

If you have an in-law in less fortunate circumstances than Molly, please be sure that you carefully explore government, religious, and family resources before you assume that you are the only one that can take care of them. There are many more resources available now than ever before. Provide reassurance, but be open about your limits. Moving an in-law into your house may sometimes be the only available option, but for obvious reasons, it could be considered only after you've explored every other choice.

WHEN THEY PULL OUT THE BIG GUNS

One thing you can count on is that as you, with or without your partner, tell your in-laws what's bothering you and how you would like it to change, you'll almost certainly be catching them off-guard. Whatever your typical way of dealing with them has been—false smiles, angry retorts, sulking, compliance—they're used to your behaving in predictable ways. Your new directness and nondefensiveness may feel very threatening to them, so don't be surprised if they pull out all the stops to try and get you back into your familiar role. It is entirely possible that you may not get apologies, validation, acknowledgment, acceptance of responsibility, or any of the wonderful things you'd like. In fact, you may get just the opposite: anger, tears, denial, projection of blame back onto you, and everything in between.

You may run into an onslaught when you talk to your in-laws. Here are some techniques they're likely to use when they feel cornered, along with some effective ways for you to respond.

1. Our Old Friend, Denial.

Your in-laws will say it never happened and you're imagining things. If, by any chance, they do acknowledge some of what you're saying, they may use an even more subtle form of denial, which goes like this: "Yes, it happened, but you're blowing it out of proportion." They will try to minimize the seriousness of their behavior by telling you you're either exaggerating, hypersensitive, or making a mountain out of a molehill.

Your Response: I realize that you don't see things as I do, we're different people and we experience things differently. But just because you say it didn't happen, doesn't mean it didn't. It happened. And what happened was very painful for me, and we're not going to get very far if you toss it off by telling me I'm exaggerating.

2. The Victim/Martyr Defense.

Here, your in-laws will say things like: "How can you do this to me/us? Why are you trying to hurt me/us like this? Why are you trying to break up this family? How can you say such things after all we've done for you?" Or they might not say much and just sigh deeply as the tears stream down their faces. Either way, you must fight being cast as the villain and giving in to your guilt.

Your Response: I'm sorry this is so upsetting to you, but I've been pretty upset for a long time, too. I have no desire to hurt you, but I need to do this for my own well-being. I appreciate the things you've done for us, but let's see if we can get past feeling sorry for ourselves to work out a better relationship.

3. You're the Problem.

Sooner or later, the blame will most likely get shifted to you. You may hear things like: "You've always been a trouble-maker," "You've never liked us," "You're impossible to get along with," " You're so neurotic," "We got along fine until you came into the picture."

Note: This one is tricky, because you have to find the fine line between taking responsibility for your own behavior that may have intensified the struggle between you, while at the same time not accepting that everything is your fault. Your in-laws may have some legitimate complaints about you, which you can acknowledge and agree to change. On the other hand, don't be too quick to accept negative labels without examining their validity. Watch out for scapegoating. Sometimes your contribution to the problems may not involve any major unpleasant behavior on your part but rather your willingness to accept what they were doing and being too fearful to deal with the problems when they first started.

Your Response: I'm sure that's the way you see it, but I'm only willing to accept fifty percent of the responsibility for why we don't get along. Perhaps you can give me some examples of things I've said or done that bothered you. I'll work on my behavior. Are you willing to do the same with yours?

4. The Best Defense Is a Good Offense.

Your in-laws may interrupt, contradict, and not give you a chance to say what you need to. They may launch an all-out attack in order to keep you from putting them on the spot.

Your Response: I'd really appreciate it if you'd hear me out. When I'm finished you can have all the time you want to respond. Otherwise, we'd better do this another time, when you're calmer.

It's impossible to cover every conceivable response, but once you get into the habit of answering firmly and nondefensively, you'll be able to apply those skills to just about every situation. The words may change, but the basic music will remain steady.

SOMETIMES NOTHING GETS RESOLVED

Many of the couples you've seen in this book had outcomes with their in-laws that ranged from a minimal, begrudging change to significant changes. Although I believe strongly in doing everything you can to try and resolve a painful situation, please bear in mind that there are some people you simply cannot get through to, no matter how skillful and articulate you may be. Some people are just impossible. They lack the capacity for any negotiations or compromise. They will see any attempt to resolve your differences as an attack and immediately counterattack. They may yell, and they may hurl accusations and insults. They will erect concrete walls to defend themselves. Once behind their barricades, they won't listen, they won't hear, and they certainly won't look at their own behavior even for a moment. They may get up and leave, slamming the door behind them.

This is their failure, not yours. If this describes your situation after you've used all your new skills and strategies, then you and your partner have some important decisions to make about how much contact you can have with people like this and still have a healthy marriage.

HOLD TO YOUR TRUTH

You never know what the ultimate outcome of facing your in-laws will be. As you saw with several of the couples in this chapter, sometimes an encounter that looks disastrous can, with time, turn around and result in some totally unexpected healing. Sometimes, of course, depending on the people you're dealing with, the opposite will happen and you may find yourself more estranged than ever. But you cannot focus on the outcome. You can only focus on what is healthy and truthful for you. Not everyone likes it when you tell the truth, but the truth needs to be told, and as long as you're respectful, you are not responsible for how other people respond to your truth.

Epilogue

For all of you who have come with me on this difficult path toward change, I'd like to remind you of the real prizes that come with this work, even if the warm embrace of your in-laws remains elusive:

- **Your life is better now.**
  I know that some or many of you did not get the apologies, acknowledgments, or the changes in your in-laws' behavior that you were hoping for. But I also know that much of your life is significantly better now. You found the courage to take on your in-law problems, and resentment and confused loyalties play a much smaller role than they did before.
- **Your marriage is stronger.**
  You and your partner, with few exceptions, are a team. You have repaired the bond that was fraying at the edges. To

rediscover and rebuild the love and loyalty of your partner is an invaluable gift, and one you have certainly earned.

- **You've regained your self-respect.**
  As soon as you stopped suffering in silence or raging in to the wind and learned to air your grievances and claim your rights, you stepped into full adulthood. It was a rite of passage as significant as any you've had, including your marriage.
- **You found your voice.**
  No one can take away the skills and strategies that are now at your fingertips, and you'll rarely be at a loss for words again. You've learned to ask for what you want with a calm assurance, and you've learned methods of communication that will serve you well in any life situation.

It may not be the fairy-tale ending in which toxic in-laws magically turn kind and loving. But you've won all the prizes just the same. You've reconnected with the person you love and, most importantly, with yourself. You've done well.

Index

29151305R00178

Made in the USA
Lexington, KY
14 January 2014